Knowledge Management

An introduction to creating competitive advantage from intellectual capital

Knowledge Management

An introduction to creating competitive advantage from intellectual capital

CARL DAVIDSON
AND PHILIP VOSS

TANDEM PRESS

To Ann and Brian Davidson:
For teaching Carl the value of knowledge from
an early age, and the merit of managing it wisely.

To Keri Woods:
The (All) Knowing Edge.

First published in New Zealand in 2002 by
Tandem Press
2A Rugby Road
Birkenhead, Auckland
New Zealand
www.tandempress.co.nz

Copyright © 2002 Carl Davidson and Philip Voss

All rights reserved. No part of this publication
may be reproduced, stored in a retrieval system
or transmitted in any form or by any means
electronic, mechanical, photocopying,
recording or otherwise without the prior
written permission of the publishers.

National Library of New Zealand Cataloguing-in-Publication Data
Davidson, Carl.
Knowledge management: an introduction to creating competitive advantage from
intellectual capital / Carl Davidson and Philip Voss.
Includes bibliographical references and index.

ISBN 1-877178-94-2

1. Knowledge management. I. Voss, Philip. II. Title
658.4038—dc 21

Cover design by Magma Design Ltd.
Text design by Verso Visual Communications.
Production by **BookNZ**
Printed in New Zealand by Publishing Press Ltd.

Acknowledgements

Knowledge management is about recognising the intellectual assets available in any organisation, and then finding a way to awaken and apply those assets in the most appropriate way possible. As such, it would be inappropriate to introduce a book on knowledge management without also acknowledging the many intellectual assets we have drawn on in writing it – or, indeed, all those people who have shared freely of their knowledge with us.

First of all, we would like to acknowledge the contribution of Trevor Williamson. Trevor, with whom we work on knowledge management projects in the Auckland market under the trading name of KM Solutions, should by all rights be the third author of this book. Certainly many of the good ideas reproduced here are his, and many more have been tested in our ongoing discussions with him. That Trevor isn't the third author is a testament to both his aversion to writing and his frustration with the post-Apple world of Windows 2000.

Speaking of the KM Solutions connection, we would also like to acknowledge all the organisations we have worked with on knowledge management projects, and to recognise how much our own thinking has changed the more we 'do' knowledge management. There is nothing like doing it to learn about it. Equally, we would like to acknowledge everyone we have taught about knowledge management in one of our executive education short courses or MBA classes. It was not for nothing that Claude Lévi-Strauss insisted that 'the wise man is not the man who gives the right answers; he is the one who asks the right questions'.

We would like to thank Christien Winter for her continuing encouragement and support. She is a *de facto* mentor, in the best possible way. Speaking of mentors, Ian Taylor (who also wrote the *Preface* for this book) and Warren Mearns continue to be touchstones for our company, No Doubt Research.

Next we would like to acknowledge all of those people who have helped us develop our ideas about knowledge management. Some of the following people have done this explicitly whereas others are probably unaware of the contributions they have made to our thinking. But just because it involves lunch or coffee doesn't mean it's not work! A far from exhaustive list would include: Andrew Barney; Steve Corbett; Jenny Darroch; Simon Davidson; Bernie Frey; Mike Groves; Neil Lunt; Vicki Jayne; Kate McKegg; Heather Mabin; Roger Matthews; John Murphy; Craig Newbury; Phil Rae; Lt Cmdr Ian Ris; Professor Paul Spoonley; Paul Stevenson; Kieran Turner; Susie Weaver; and Colm Whyte. Tanya Zorlu gets a special mention for telling us about different learning styles and multiple intelligences, and pointing us in the direction of Howard Gardner's work.

We also want to acknowledge all those writers who have helped shape our thinking about knowledge management. Even though we have never met them, we would like to acknowledge the contribution of John Seely Brown, Thomas Davenport, Stephen Denning, Paul Duguid, Charles Jonscher, Larry Prusak, David Shenk, Thomas Stewart, and Edward Tenner.

Turning all of our good ideas into a book required both the enduring faith of a publisher, and the guiding hand of a good editor. Bob Ross of Tandem Press provided the first, and in spades. We have been involved in a number of book projects over the years but neither of us can remember one as straightforward as this. Thanks Bob. Joan Havemann edited the manuscript (in record time) and, in the process, helped us both become more effective writers. Joan's background in management communication also meant she provided us with a useful and interesting commentary on the manuscript.

Finally, we need to thank our families and loved ones for supporting us through the many late nights and weekends that made up this book. Carl would especially like to thank Amy Allen, who apart from being tremendously understanding during that writing, also worked to rid the early drafts of their many anacolutha. A remarkable achievement, when you consider that – as she is from Florida – English really is a second language to her. Philip would like to give special thanks to his fiancée, Keri Woods, for being there when needed, as always; and to his baby son, Kieran, who is a joy to us all as well as the most fascinating and adorable knowledge management project we've yet been involved with.

January, 2002

Contents

	Foreword	9
	Introduction	11
(1)	Knowledge as Power: What is the Knowledge Economy?	17
(2)	Why You Need to Know about Knowledge Management	31
(3)	Knowledge Management 101	50
(4)	Drowning in Information?	69
(5)	Successful Knowledge Management	88
(6)	Knowledge Management in Action	114
(7)	The Mature Knowledge-Managing Organisation	141
(8)	Getting Started Tomorrow	162
	Notes	173
	Glossary	175
	References	183
	Index	189

Foreword

*Ask me what is the most important thing
And I will reply
It is people,
It is people,
It is people.*
– MAORI PROVERB

This proverb, used as the insightful parting thought of *Knowledge Management*, can be refined for the workplace of the twenty-first century by Tom Peters's observation that 'heavy lifting is out; brains are in'. This is perhaps nowhere more obvious than in how industrial businesses are attempting to transform themselves from 'physical asset rich' to 'intangible asset rich' – Monsanto from commodity chemicals to life sciences; General Electric from manufacturing to services; and Westinghouse from whitegoods to media/high-tech. At the heart of these, and similar change processes, is the immutable truth that people determine the success of any technology or knowledge development.

It is the quality of human capital, in terms of creativity, insight, entrepreneurship and innovation, that is the source of an organisation's, or a country's, competitive advantage. Bid fond farewell to the value chain and embrace the value network!

Carl and Philip's book is timely, not only for knowledge management as a discipline, but for New Zealand as a nation. The collective consciousness of our country is more acutely aware now, than ever before, of the new era in which the rules of commerce are being rewritten. The new knowledge-based business model is revolutionising roles, requiring new competencies, reshaping value creation, redesigning the employer–employee relationship, and drastically recasting accounting models to include human capital.

In this book the case for smart knowledge management is succinct, taut and well researched. Beyond this, though, the book provides substantial practical insight based on a wealth of field and consulting experience unique in this part of the world. It is this broad, pragmatic and multidimensional recipe that should satisfy both the demanding academic and hard-headed practitioner.

Beyond these more prescriptive demands, the sharp wit and astute anecdotal observations of the authors make this, in the most genuine sense, an interesting and compelling read.

Indeed, it is part of the empire of two very good minds.

Ian Taylor
Managing Principal, Sheffield Consulting

Introduction

There is no greater power on Earth than an idea whose time has come.
– VICTOR HUGO

Why Knowledge Management?

The thesis of this book can be summed up in two simple maxims: The first takes Francis Bacon's famous idea that 'knowledge itself is power' and tells us that, in the 'new economy' of the twenty-first century, we have moved to a world where knowledge *sharing* is power. The second draws from a poster one of the authors saw on an office wall many years ago, which said:

> **Computers: Fast. Accurate.** *Dumb.*
> **People: Slow. Sloppy.** *Smart.*

Taken together, these two ideas tell us that the pre-eminent source of competitive advantage ('power') in the modern economy comes from the sharing of knowledge, and that the source of that knowledge is people. As a simple summary of knowledge management, that's as good as any. A more conventional summary would say that knowledge management is about

> **creating systems that enable organisations to tap into the knowledge, experiences, and creativity of their staff to improve their performance.**

We like this definition because it makes it clear that knowledge management is about sharing knowledge, not for its own sake, but rather as a means to discover ways that enable staff to carry out business processes faster, better, and at lower costs. Knowledge management starts from an assumption that the way to thrive in the contemporary economy is for organisations to work smarter. But note that we did not say 'work smarter *rather* than harder', precisely because sometimes the smartest things to do involve a redoubling of effort. This is an important point, if only to highlight the fact that knowledge management is not a soft option — it is not about 'touchy-feely' talkfests designed simply so your staff can share their inner fears. Knowledge management is fundamentally purposive. Sharing knowledge becomes a source of competitive advantage only to those organisations that enable staff to *learn* how to do their jobs better and then ensure they *do* them better. In other words, if your approach to knowledge management does not improve how your organisation performs over time, then you are doing something wrong.

Although there is unlikely to be much disagreement that the source of competitive advantage has changed considerably in recent years (with inventiveness replacing inventory), it takes more than this agreement to recognise knowledge for the corporate asset it is. Said another way, few companies realise the potential rewards of knowledge because they misunderstand what it is and what they need to do to gain control of it. The Standards Australia report *International Best Practice: Case Studies in Knowledge Management* (2001) identifies five common symptoms showing that knowledge is managed poorly in an organisation:

- Knowledge creation, transmission, and use remain unstructured (and hence, informal and often unconscious processes).
- Decisions are often made without the benefit of the best knowledge available to the organisation.
- Knowledge is not reused or shared, meaning staff either continually reinvent the wheel or duplicate the efforts of others elsewhere in the organisation.
- People are overwhelmed with information that detracts from, rather than adds to, their ability to do their job (paradoxically, creating a situation where staff experience a simultaneous flood and drought of information).
- Knowledge hoarding by staff is common, and there is little organisational interest in the value of developing knowledge capacity among staff.

The fact that these symptoms are widespread makes it clear that, although there is nothing new about knowledge per se, recognising it as a corporate asset continues to challenge many organisations. This book argues that what organisations require is more than a casual (or even unconscious) approach to managing that knowledge.

The emphasis on 'improving organisational performance through learning' introduces another important dimension to knowledge management too. Knowledge that drives the learning in any organisation can just as readily be sourced outside that organisation as within it. Knowledge management is about bringing the most useful knowledge you can find to assist in solving the kinds of problems the organisation faces on a regular basis – and in pre-empting the kinds of problems the organisation is likely to confront in the future.

It is because there is likely to be so much knowledge that could potentially be useful to any organisation that information technologies are seen by some people as the key to knowledge management.

This is understandable when you think about how rapidly the amount of information around us grows. We have all heard the stories about how the volume of information in the world doubles every 10 to 20 years, or how more information has been produced in the 50 years since the end of World War Two than in the two thousand years leading up to it. Surely computers are better at managing this clutter than are staff? Our answer to that question may surprise you: we are big fans of computers, and certainly recognise that they play an important role in helping manage knowledge. However, we also think that far too much has been made of that role and altogether too little made about creating the conditions where staff are excited about sharing what they know and about learning from the experiences of others.

In short, we think computers do help with knowledge management but only once we are very clear about how they support sharing and learning in any organisational context. It is very important that debates about knowledge management are not simply reduced to arguments about the latest hardware, software, or groupware offering. Knowledge management is about organisational learning and about organisational thinking. Except, of course, organisations don't ever really learn or think – only the people who work for them can do that. This is especially important in the information economy of the twenty-first century where, as one wit put it, there are data, data everywhere, but not a thought to think.

In sum, this book will argue that managing knowledge is far more about how organisations manage their staff than it is about how much they spend on information technology. This may make more sense when we reflect that knowledge management (and the improved organisational performance it promises) is all about creating organisational processes that fulfil four essential functions:

1. **identification** of the key knowledge assets that exist in your organisation;
2. **reflection** about what your organisation knows (and, by extension, what it doesn't know);
3. **sharing** that knowledge with whoever needs to know it; and
4. **applying** that knowledge to improve the way your organisation performs.

We have deliberately set out to provide an *introduction* to knowledge management. This book is designed to be read by those curious about what knowledge management is, what it might offer their organisation, and how they can get started. It is not designed to be a comprehensive summary of the (increasingly vast) literature on knowledge management, nor is it designed to provide the last word on what any particular organisation should do to manage knowledge. It is our firm belief, drawn from our considerable experience working in the field of knowledge management, that **there is no simple recipe for successful knowledge management**. Different organisations will need to generate their own in-house recipes from their own experiences. This book will provide some important pointers on what ingredients those recipes will involve, and even on how to prepare them, but the final result will necessarily differ from organisation to organisation. And, as the old adage has it, in all cases the diners and not the cook shall be the ones who judge the quality of the meal.

The Structure of this Book

Teachers open the door, but you must enter by yourself.
- CHINESE PROVERB

As an introduction to knowledge management, this book works from the general – What is the knowledge economy? Why do you need to know about knowledge management? What is the key to successful knowledge management? – through to the specific – What methods can you use to manage knowledge? What can you do to get started on knowledge management tomorrow?

The first chapter, 'Knowledge as Power: What is the Knowledge Economy?' examines why knowledge has become the pre-eminent source of competitive advantage in the twenty-first century. It considers the arguments for the new economy and discusses what is really meant by the 'information revolution'. This chapter asks how the ground rules of economic competition have shifted in recent years, and what this means for the way organisations operate.

Chapter two, 'Why You Need to Know about Knowledge Management', defines what knowledge management is, outlines why you need to know about it, and talks about where and when organisations should apply it. This chapter argues that knowledge management provides a key tool for organisations attempting to adapt to the new rules of economic competition. It also outlines why traditional approaches to accounting and economics mean many organisations have overlooked the potential value of the 'brain gain' available to them.

The third chapter, 'Knowledge Management 101', outlines the basic concepts used in every discussion about knowledge management and prepares the reader for the arguments to follow. Before you read beyond this chapter, it is important you are comfortable with the hierarchy of data, information, and knowledge, as well as with the differences between structural, human, and customer/supplier capital and between tacit and explicit knowledge. You'll be reading a lot about those ideas from this point on.

Chapter four, 'Drowning in Information?' explains why knowledge management is more about HR (human resources) than IT (information technologies). It emphasises the role that learning plays in knowledge management, and talks about the appropriate roles that computers can play in supporting that learning. The chapter talks about the limitations of computers specifically, and technology in general, in creating learning communities. In essence, in this chapter we argue that knowledge management needs to be concerned with the quality of information, not the quantity, and with the timeliness of information delivery, not its speed.

In chapter five, 'Successful Knowledge Management', we develop our ideas about what distinguishes successful knowledge management strategies. In chapter four, we argue that knowledge management is about more than impressive computing architectures, and here we outline what those extra elements are. This chapter identifies three critical components to knowledge management (the right knowledge streams and sources feeding into the organisation; the right technology to store and communicate that knowledge; and the right workplace culture so that staff are motivated to make use of that knowledge) and talks about how many organisations concentrate their efforts in only one of these areas. The key point here is that successful knowledge management can only occur at the intersection of all three of the areas identified.

Having established what knowledge management is, why your organisation needs to know about it, and the key to developing a successful strategy to manage knowledge, chapter six, 'Knowledge Management in Action', outlines how to get started. It introduces a methodology to fulfil the four essential functions identified above, outlines the goals of each of the steps, and provides guidelines about how to realise those goals. As already noted, these are necessarily guidelines, because the only way to discover which specific methods actually work in any organisational context is to trial a range of them in some kind of initial knowledge management project. From this necessity comes another important recommendation – that you approach knowledge management cautiously. Pilot schemes and case studies provide a useful means to identify the methods that will work best in your own organisation. To attempt a widespread approach without having first identified the most appropriate methods simply increases the chances of failure.

The approach outlined in chapter six is designed to get organisations started out with knowledge management. Chapter seven, 'The Mature Knowledge-Managing Organisation', reflects on what an organisation would look like if it embedded the four essential functions as part of its everyday operation. The implicit argument here is that, where it is taken seriously, knowledge management has the potential to transform an organisation beyond recognition.

The final chapter, 'Getting Started Tomorrow', provides a list of simple suggestions your organisation could use tomorrow to begin managing knowledge. These ideas are deliberately low-cost options, hence providing a soft entry into the field of knowledge management. The broader philosophy of this chapter is reflected in a theme that runs throughout the entire book: that the best way to assess whether knowledge management is for you is try it and see. By starting small, and drawing on the resources already in your organisation, the downside risk to such experimentation can easily be limited.

The last thing we want to say about the structure of the book is that it builds its argument incrementally. Although individual chapters may just about stand on their own (should you have specific questions about knowledge management from the outset), each chapter is written to take you a little further down the path towards knowledge management. It makes sense to read the chapters sequentially.

chapter one

Knowledge as Power: What is the Knowledge Economy?

The most successful businessman is the man who holds onto the old just as long as it is good, and grabs the new just as soon as it is better.
– LEE IACOCCA

Children of the Revolution?

The central premise of this book is that the ground rules of economic competition have shifted in important ways in recent years. As a result, organisations need to adapt to these new rules if they are to survive and thrive in this new environment. Most of this book concerns itself with what we see as the key tool for organisational adaptation to this new environment – knowledge management. Because the book is written by two social scientists, it will argue that the secret to successful knowledge management is in what John Seely Brown and Paul Duguid have called the social life of information. In short, our thesis is that managing knowledge is far more about how organisations manage their staff than it is about how much they spend on information technology. 'Knowledge management' may sound dauntingly high-tech but it is sometimes as simple as getting people from different parts of the organisation to start talking to each other. Before we do that, however, we want to establish why we think the ground rules of economic competition have shifted in important ways in recent years.

An obvious place to start is with the popular use (and overuse) of such labels as the information economy, e-commerce, the learning organisation, or the knowledge worker. Indeed, it would have taken a heroic effort to have avoided any of these labels in recent years – be it in the media, at one kind of management seminar or another, over lunch, or listening to your children discussing their homework. To take a noticeable example, questions about how to build competitive advantage in the knowledge economy dominated policy debates in the recent elections in the USA (2000) and the UK (2001), as well as in New Zealand (2002). The flavour of many of these commentaries is best captured by the breathless enthusiasm of *Wired* magazine's *Encyclopedia of the New Economy*, which tells us that 'when we talk about the new economy, we're talking about a world in which people work with their brains instead of their hands ... a world so different its emergence can only be described as a revolution' (http://hotwired.lycos.com/special/ene/). The sheer volume of time and space dedicated to these issues is one clear indicator that a great many important people think that something important is going on. But how do we know it is not simply hype?

This is not a frivolous question. You do not need to be a wizened cynic to realise that neither the media nor politicians (and especially those seeking re-election) are the most dispassionate or objective observers of social and economic trends. To argue that any trend is 'real' simply because either of these groups insist it is would be remarkably naïve. The important question, then, is not 'Who says that the knowledge economy is real?' but 'How do they know that it is?' Fortunately, there is considerable evidence that this trend is much more than the product of media hype or political spin.

For instance, research carried out by Ernst and Young in 1999 demonstrated that more than 50 per cent of the Gross Domestic Product (GDP) in the major OECD (Organization for Economic Cooperation and Development) economies was based on the production and distribution of knowledge. The World Bank, in the same year, wrote in its *World Development Report*:

> For countries in the vanguard of the world economy, the balance between knowledge and resources has shifted so far towards the former that knowledge had become perhaps the most important factor determining the standard of living – more than land, than tools, than labour.

Alan Greenspan has similarly argued that 'over half of US economic growth is associated with the growth of its knowledge based economy.' David Shenk tells us that by the year 2000 the 'information superhighway' was supposed to be generating US$1 trillion in revenue, 'making it the largest industrial sector in the world'.

But the real evidence for the rise in the importance of knowledge is even more immediate than this. As Charles Leadbeater has noted, in 1910 the world's 10 biggest companies sold products you could stand inside. Today, the value of the top 10 companies 'lives in programming code, in tiny pills packed with scientific knowledge, in The Brand. In Weightlessness' (Philp, 2001:26). Equally, consider the two well-known examples of (i) the personal wealth of Bill Gates, and (ii) the market capitalisation of Microsoft. Bill Gates, as any schoolchild will tell you, is the richest person in the world. Yet this fortune was not amassed by owning oil wells, or inheriting vast tracts of real estate, or running guns, or any of the other traditionally respectable ways that robber barons made serious amounts of money. Bill Gates became that rich by creating a company that designed software products that simply took over the world. In 1999, Microsoft Inc. was worth more on the stock exchange than the entire US automobile industry (Jonscher, 2000:5). These two facts alone are testament to how radically the fabric of capitalism has changed in recent years.

Equally, the largest merger in American corporate history involved America-On-Line (AOL) and Time Warner. The logic of the merger was a relatively simple one: essentially, AOL would provide Time Warner with the bandwidth to transmit their content to new customers, while Time Warner would provide the content that AOL needed to expand their services. Of course, the real value in this merger was seen in the synergies (a word we will be hearing more of in this book) that would emerge over time. The important point for our purposes here is that the size of the merger underscores the value that the world's most developed economy has come to place on information.

Precisely how much value, and what exactly is being valued, is also important for our discussion. Before the dotcom bubble deflated, Charles Jonscher tells us, AOL boasted a market capitalisation of some US$25 billion, in stark contrast to its book value of 'merely' US$125 million. In other words, the market had valued the company at 200 times what its tangible assets were worth. And this was a story that was repeated throughout those organisations on the 'knowing edge' of the US economy in the 1990s.

Now, for sure, some of that extra value was the product of investor exuberance. But – and this is the important point – not all of it was. Today many of the companies at the knowing edge of the US economy maintain a market capitalisation above their book value. The dotcom bubble deflated but it did not burst. The reason it did not burst for many of these companies is that investors were on to an important shift in how organisations build and maintain competitive advantage. That is, the way these companies create wealth has precious little to do with the physical assets they own and almost everything to do with the people who work for them and the systems they have in place to enable these people to be creative and innovative. In the words of *Wired* magazine, 'most of [Microsoft's] assets walk in and out of the doors wearing T-shirts.'

Thomas Stewart, in his landmark book, *Intellectual Capital*, compared Microsoft with IBM to demonstrate the value the market has come to place on these intangible assets 'wearing T-shirts'. A quick check on the Network World 200 (NW200) database reveals that many of these numbers have since changed, but the point about the relative value of intangible and tangible assets remains. Stewart tells us that, as of November 1996, IBM had a total market capitalisation of US$70.7 billion compared to Microsoft's US$85.5 despite the fact that:

- IBM had sales more than fifteen times those of Microsoft
- IBM's software business alone generated more sales than all of Microsoft
- in that year, IBM owned US$16.6 billion worth of property, plant and equipment, whereas Microsoft owned 'just' US$930 million.

To reiterate how bizarre (on face value at least) this discrepancy in market capitalisation is, Stewart notes that, in 1996, every $100 invested in IBM bought the lucky investor $23 worth of fixed assets whereas the same $100 invested in Microsoft bought only $1's worth. So what exactly is it that you buy when you buy Microsoft? Why would any sane investor spend 99 of their hard-earned dollars on something they couldn't see? Interestingly, there is a story that suggests Bill Gates and Paul Allen answered that question during the company's initial public offering (IPO) in 1986. As Paul Toutonghi recites it, the Microsoft accountants were anxious because the company seemed overvalued and an inaccurate market capitalisation would drive the stock through the floor. The accountants argued that they couldn't find the value to support the capitalisation estimate and the numbers were 'all wrong'. According to Toutonghi, Gates is supposed to have replied 'The value is right here', tapping his head, 'here, in us, in the people, in the code we can write. We're the value of the corporation' (Toutonghi, 2000). It's a good story, probably even too good to be true, but it captures an important point. No-one invests in Microsoft, or any of the other 'knowing edge' companies, because of the value of their traditional assets. Instead, what you buy is the *ability* of the company to do innovative and creative things. In many cases, as witnessed in the dotcom phenomenon, what investors are buying is not even the ability to do those things but the *apparent promise* of the ability to do those things.

To take another example, when IBM bought Lotus in 1995, it paid US$3.5 billion for a company with a book value of US$250 million. As Thomas Davenport and Laurence Prusak tell us:

> IBM did not pay that amount of money for the current revenue generated by Notes and other Lotus products or for Lotus's manufacturing and sales capabilities ... the $3.25 billion premium IBM paid represents their appraisal of Lotus's unique knowledge ... the minds that invented Notes are more valuable than the software itself.

The sheer size of the premium paid represents what can be thought of as 'the brain gain' – the value inside an organisation that can be unlocked if you can get your staff 'to work with their brains as well as their hands' (Davenport and Prusak, 1998). When a stock market values a company at a number of times the book value of its assets, it is telling a simple but profound truth. And, this book will argue, it is a truth we are now hearing everywhere. A study carried out by Professor Baruch Lev of New York University's Stern School of Business examined the accounts of thousands of US companies over a 20-year period. The study concluded that, by the mid-1990s, traditional book assets accounted for perhaps as little as 20 per cent of the stock market value of those companies (Leadbeater, 2000:47).

As we will see, the reason that many organisations have not yet realised the magnitude of their own potential brain gain is that they have not had the tools to do so. This shift, away from tangible assets that are easy to value towards intangible assets that are notoriously difficult to value, is one that has caused major problems for conventional economics and accounting practices. For companies that are not listed on the stock market, the problem is the same one that Microsoft faced before its 1986 IPO: the conventional suite of accounting figures simply cannot reflect the real value available in the organisation. This point is perhaps best illustrated by the fact that some enormously successful companies, such as Visa or Netscape, have almost no tangible assets whatsoever.

It is precisely because investors (and smart organisations) *have* started to appreciate the link between their intangible assets and their bottom line that so many media commentators (and politicians) are falling over themselves to claim that this is the era of the knowledge economy. Thomas Stewart, as have many after him, has gone so far as to say that the shift to 'the information age' will be as profound as the changes wrought by the industrial revolution; that what we are experiencing is indeed our own 'revolution' where 'business, economic life, and society itself, are all being reinvented.' Stewart uses the example of the microchip to illustrate the nature of the changes going on in advanced economies. First, he notes that the value of microchips produced in the world has overtaken the value of steel. Second, he points out that the raw ingredient of microchips — silicone — comes from sand. And there isn't even much of that. Instead, the real value of these chips comes from their design and the design of the machines that make them. The value is in the intellectual content, not the physical. The microchip is a wonderful symbol of the information revolution because, as Stewart points out, it demonstrates clearly how manufacturing will become increasingly like a professional service. If you think about the cost of hiring a lawyer for an hour then it is obvious that very little of the fee goes to pay for physical overheads. Most of it goes to pay for the brainpower of the lawyer. Stewart uses Brian Arthur's notion of 'congealed knowledge' to capture this shift. In the old economy, we are told, people bought 'congealed resources' — a lot of material held together by a little knowledge. In today's economy they buy congealed knowledge — a little material held together by a lot of knowledge. Peter Drucker picks up a similar theme in his *Managing in a Time of Great Change* (1997) when he says that 'knowledge has become the key economic resource and the dominant — and perhaps the only — source of competitive advantage.'

A NEW ZEALAND PERSPECTIVE

For New Zealand, the rise of information technology and networks provides especially attractive opportunities. By overcoming the old tyranny of distance, these technologies provide a mechanism for surmounting our remoteness from world markets. As the Information Technology Advisory Group (ITAG) put it, 'the Internet is the modern equivalent of the freezer ship that revolutionised our economy last century' (1999:2). We don't know how much of New Zealand's GDP comes from knowledge — our official statistics do not currently let us extrapolate such data. The best we can do is note that the IT sector accounts for 7 per cent of our GDP (ITAG, 1999:2). The point has been made above, however, that knowledge is *the* key to New Zealand's future economic prosperity. Our competitors are now playing a very different game, and one whose rules New Zealand companies are yet to fully learn.

Yet, in the memorable words of the ITAG report, 'If New Zealanders do not seize the opportunities provided by the knowledge economy, we will survive only as an amusement park and holiday land for citizens from more successful economies' (1999:2). The challenge is for local companies 'to better understand and use the concept of intellectual capital ... to look at their products, processes, and people, and assess and augment the amount of knowledge they possess' (1999:7).

Revolution or Uprising? How Revolutionary is Information, Really?

'Would you — be good enough', Alice panted out, after running a little further,
'to stop a minute just to get one's breath again?'
'I'm good enough', the King said, 'only I'm not strong enough.
You see, a minute goes by so fearfully quick.'
- LEWIS CARROLL, *THROUGH THE LOOKING GLASS*

Although we agree that knowledge has indeed become an important source of (often overlooked) competitive advantage, we are much more sceptical that we are living in a time of real revolution. We tend to agree with John Seely Brown and Paul Duguid when they make the point that predictions about the future are often made by people extrapolating from those out on the leading edge of social and technical change. Surrounded by such 'early adopters', and carried away with their own breathless enthusiasm, it is easy for such users to mistake 'could' for 'should'. We all know the kind of evangelists of change we are talking about here, the kind of user who, seduced by the sheer functionality of technology, assumes other users will rise to that level of proficiency.

By contrast, our assessment of the information revolution is somewhat more modest. Although we accept that there will be a group of people for whom the world will be changed beyond all recognition (and, moreover, in ways that are difficult to predict or even fathom), for the majority of us the changes will occur in terms of how we do the things that we have always done. As our friend and colleague Neil Lunt, an expert in evaluation research, repeatedly points out, most researchers and writers are drawn to change. Change is sexy if only for the simple reason that something can be seen to be happening. In John Seely Brown and Paul Duguid's memorable phrase, 'we notice the ripple but take the lake for granted' (2000:138). The more change, and the faster it happens, the better for those who wish to document it. What this approach lacks, of course, is any consideration of those things in our lives that stubbornly remain the same.

To take one simple example, both the authors are regular users of the online bookstore Amazon.com. There is little doubt that the availability of this service has added to our shopping experience in useful ways – for instance, through the ability to shop at any time of the day or night (and to do it wearing whatever – or as little – as we want). We are often sent e-mails from friends and colleagues drawing our attention to a book, and we are then able to order it from Amazon.com without leaving our desks. There is little doubt that there are times when this ability is profoundly convenient. And yet, none of this changes the way that books are written or printed, nor does it obviate the need for someone to find the book we have ordered on a warehouse shelf, pack it, and dispatch it to us. The books still turn up at our door and, once read, are safely stored on our bookshelves. Furthermore, being able to access Amazon.com has not stopped either of us visiting 'real' bookshops, or whiling away pleasant afternoons in second-hand bookshops. We are both fully aware that e-books exist and are seen by many people as an alternative to 'real' books. But such books will never replace their 'real' counterparts for either of us. There are many good reasons why, but the larger point is that full-time access to the Internet has not changed our relationship to books, or even bookshops, in any significant way. Finally, as John Seely Brown and Paul Duguid note (2000:46), there is also a wonderful irony in the fact that the 'first great flagship of the Internet,' Amazon.com, is a bookshop. Books are the oldest of all manufactured commodities, and they are wonderfully standardised products.

Our collective experiences with Amazon.com are a microcosm of a much broader phenomenon – namely that information technologies have simply not changed our lives as much as we were once told they would. A paperless office, anyone? A leisure society? Telecommuting as a solution to wasting time stuck in traffic? Both Charles Jonscher (2000) and Edward Tenner (1997) do a better job than most of explaining why technology rarely works as its promoters promise and, ironically, often ends up changing our lives in ways that no-one ever predicted. In chapter four, we will see what this means for the practice of knowledge management, but the point being made here is that there is an increasing awareness of what has been called the productivity paradox: that there is little relationship between investment in information technology and productivity gains. It is a point captured most famously by Robert

Solow, the Nobel Laureate economist from MIT, who noted that 'we see computers everywhere except in the productivity statistics' (in Jonscher, 2000:189). To social scientists, the relative failure of information technology to deliver immediate, and profound, productivity gains is no surprise. We often find ourselves having to remind people that information technology merely provides the tools for people to *do* things with. In contrast to the technological determinism of many proponents ('You must buy this because it will change your life'), we are firm believers in what we would once have called the 'social construction' of technology ('How can I use and adapt this to meet my existing needs?').

To take one of our favourite examples: although it is now the case that the microchips built into new cars are worth more than the steel they make the car out of (Leadbeater, 1999:9), the fact remains that those cars are just as likely to spend their lives stuck in traffic. We frivolously call this the cup-holder paradox after a true story recounted by one of our company's IT systems gurus. Enamoured with hi-tech in all its manifestations, when the time came to buy a new car he sought out one with a built-in global positioning system (GPS). This system, enabling his car to be tracked by satellites anywhere on Earth, could pinpoint its position to within a couple of metres. Of course, that car then spent most of its life stuck in traffic on the Northern Motorway into the city, where his expensive GPS system told him things he already knew (that he was stuck in traffic on the Northern Motorway and that he wasn't making much progress to his designated waypoint). By contrast, when it came time for his partner to look for a new car, her main concern was that it had sufficient cup-holders for her and the friends she shared the commute with. In her old car, where there were no cup-holders, much coffee had been spilled and many laps burned. In this regard, the fact that the new car had somewhere to put their obligatory morning coffees made a material difference to the quality of their commuting. In the social context where it would actually be used, the GPS system, for all its high tech marvel, was simply an expensive distraction – a solution in search of a problem. Whereas the cup-holders, as low tech as they might be, were the perfect solution to the needs of that group of users. This is a distinction to which we will return in chapter two because we think it is an important one for understanding successful knowledge management – simply that the key is being 'smart' rather than pursuing 'high tech'. In this case, the cup-holder was clearly the low tech solution but it was also, by far, the smarter of the two.

To return to the bigger picture, the important point is that we believe it is unlikely we are living in a time of revolution where a new economy will replace, and make redundant, the old one. Instead, the social and economic changes going on around us are much more complex and interesting than this. Patricia Hewitt, the Secretary of State for Trade and Industry (as well as the e-Minister in Cabinet) for Tony Blair's government in the UK, has argued that anyone who believes the information revolution will lead to the decline of old-economy industries, such as manufacturing, is simply 'profoundly wrong'. Seeing not so much an information 'revolution' as an 'uprising', Hewitt talks of how its effects will be felt by 'every product and service, every part of the production process and [in] every sector of the economy' (see www.dti.gov.uk). Consequently, organisations will not be made obsolete by rapid changes that obliterate their markets but, instead, will need to respond to the challenge of how to do things smarter. The idea that organisations need to work smarter has become emptied of all its meaning thanks to overuse, but the advent of the knowledge economy makes working smarter an imperative. In this race, brains beat fast-twitch muscle fibre every time.

As we will see, the implications of taking the idea of working smarter seriously are profound. The shift to making products and services smarter means companies will need to redesign the organisational structures they use to manufacture and market these products and services. There is some debate about what this means for large organisational structures but, regardless of whether giant corporations can survive, many historical or contemporary human resource management practices will necessarily become obsolete.

The Forces Driving the Information Uprising

In an economy where the only certainty is uncertainty, the one sure source of lasting competitive advantage is knowledge.
– IKUJIRO NONAKA, THE KNOWLEDGE CREATING COMPANY

Having established, in broad overview at least, that there are real imperatives driving organisations to genuinely work smarter, it may pay to trace these changes to their source. Like all important social and economic shifts, these trends are the product of a myriad of smaller and interrelated forces. However, a simplistic overview might highlight four important streams.

The Impetus of Globalisation
Here today, and next week, tomorrow!
- MR TOAD, IN KENNETH GRAHAME, *THE WIND IN THE WILLOWS*

One of our favourite descriptions of globalisation is Pico Iyer's notion that 'everywhere is [increasingly] made up of everywhere else' (2000:11). British sociologist Anthony Giddens tells us that 'in recent years globalization has been at the centre of most political discussion and economic debates' (Giddens, 1998:28). Why our generations got to experience this phenomenon — this 'polycentric amalgam' (to use another of Iyer's phrases) — has to do with developments in (and a combination of) technology and travel. Indeed, travel has become the largest industry in the world (Iyer, 2000:12). Although most aspects of globalisation are disputed (with as many definitions and descriptions as there are people writing about the subject), a simple summary might be that the rise of global markets and standards, the subsequent decline of local borders, and developments in technology and travel have all led to the opening of enormous markets. The corollary of this is that it has also exposed organisations to an equally enormous number of new competitors. Consequently, globalisation has fuelled what Robert Frank and Philip Cook (1996) label 'the winner-take-all society'. Although providing consumers with unprecedented choice, globalisation has introduced competition to organisations that is truly Darwinian in scope. Consequently, as Thomas Davenport and Laurence Prusak (1998) put it, 'companies can no longer expect that the products and practices that made them successful in the past will keep them viable in the future.'

The Proliferation of Information Technology
I think there is a world market for about five computers.
- THOMAS J WATSON, 1943 (FOUNDER, IBM)

There is no reason for any individual to have a computer in their home.
- KEN OLSON, 1977 (PRESIDENT, DIGITAL)

There is a famous 'law' among technological evangelists known as Moore's Law. This law is really an observation made by Gordon Moore, the inventor of the microchip and the founder of Intel Corporation, who noted that, with price kept constant, the processing power of microchips doubles every 18 months. It is this phenomenon (one that has proved remarkably robust to date) that has spawned the rapid growth of information technologies. Simply put, as the costs of computers have come down (according to Moore's Law, you can get the same computing power for half-price in 18 months or twice as much power for the same money), the number of applications for them has gone up. This means that all kinds of machines have got smarter (with microchips seemingly popping up everywhere from the washing machine to the hand-held personal digital assistant [PDA]), got cheaper, and sold in ever-increasing numbers. To take some examples at random: even in the late 1980s a laser printer that could approximate typeset quality sold for as much as $20,000. Today, similar quality can be had for under one thousand dollars. In 1991, the top of the range 386 Compaq desktop cost NZ$15,703, while the 486/25 model sold for a staggering $48,072 (*New Zealand PC World*, August 2001:89). The average price per megabyte for hard disks declined from more than $10 in 1988 to around two cents by 1999 (Rollo and Clarke, 2001:8). James Gleick, in *Faster: The Acceleration of Just About Everything*, recounts how sales of fax machines in the US went from 80,000 in 1984 to two million in 1989 (Gleick, 1999). Equally, Gary Hamel, in *Leading the Revolution*, recounts how mobile phone sales jumped from 26 million in 1994 to nearly 300 million by 1999 (Hamel, 2000).

Moreover, as the number of computers proliferated, so the networks tying them together grew. As the numbers of computers exceeded some critical threshold, the networks started to take on a life of their own. The importance of these networks has been called 'the second phase of the digital revolution' (Jonscher, 2000:262). This is reflected in what is known as Metcalfe's Law: 'The cost of a network expands linearly with increases in network size, but the value of a network increases exponentially.' Consequently, intranets, extranets, and the Internet have become the language of business everywhere. With the growth of networks tied to the rise of globalisation (see above), time and distance have become all but irrelevant to how certain types or aspects of business get done. In Bill Gates's memorable phrase, they now allow organisations to conduct 'business at the speed of thought' (Gates, 1999).

The Availability of Information
The desire for knowledge increases ever with the acquisition of it.
– LAURENCE STERNE

As information technologies declined in price, so information became more readily available, easier to reproduce, and easier to create. How much easier is best captured by the claim that 'more data will be created in the next three years than in the whole of human history' (*The Economist*, 9 December 2000:75). Beyond the predictions are some stunning statistics: James Gleick talks about how the number of books listed by *Books in Print* rose from 85,000 in 1947 to 1.8 million in 1998 – a 21-fold increase during a time when the US population did not quite double (Gleick, 1999). David Shenk in his book *Data Smog: Surviving the Information Glut* picks up the same point when he recounts how per capita paper consumption in the US grew from 200 pounds in 1940 to 600 pounds in 1980, and then to 1,800 pounds by 1990 (Shenk, 1997). The Pentagon alone makes 350,000 photocopies a day – about the same as a thousand decent size novels *a day* (Pratkanis and Aronson, 2000). How fast information has grown is also demonstrated by the astronomical rise of the World Wide Web. In 1997, one estimate put the number of web pages at 22 million, containing a total of 11 billion words, and by 1998 the best estimate had become 400 million pages (Shenk, 1997; Jonscher, 2000). In 2000, *The Economist* estimated that about 610 billion e-mails were sent in the USA alone each year (21 October 2000:108), while another source claimed that the worldwide volume was over four trillion (a six-fold jump between 1995 and 2001) (*NZ Business*, June 2001). Since 1998, the Internet has grown so fast that only the bravest or most foolhardy commentator would attempt to estimate how many people use it or how often. Assuredly, the number of users is growing so fast that claims date faster than a day-trader's fortunes. The consequence of this proliferation of information is that, in theory at least, facts and figures that may once have taken half a day to find in a library are now available at the fingertips of staff; memos that may never have been found in your office are a single computer file away. People are thus able to do more with information simply because they have access to so much more of it.

The Changing Nature of Organisational Forms
One machine can do the work of fifty ordinary men.
No machine can do the work of one extraordinary man.
– ELBERT HUBBARD

Throughout the 1980s, the nature and structure of work changed as organisations attempted to adjust to the changing nature of the global economy. It was almost as if every six months a new wave of change became fashionable – re-engineering, TQM, JIT inventory control, balanced scorecards, downsizing, and so on. Academics seemingly struggled to keep up with the changes, alternatively writing about 'the

New Industrial Order', 'post-Fordism', 'post-modernity', 'disorganised capitalism', or 'flexible specialisation' (to pick just a handful). These organisational changes, whatever they were called or however they were interpreted, did two important things. First, they sent a clear signal that the characteristic architecture of industrial organisation (the corporate hierarchy) was no longer working as well as it once did. Secondly, they freed a large pool of workers to look (however reluctantly) for alternatives to working for those corporations. This changing nature of work thus provided an impetus to look for alternative ways of working, and generated a large pool of workers to try those alternatives.

It is these four broad forces — the impetus of globalisation, the proliferation of information technology, the availability of information, and the changing nature of organisational forms — that drives the central premise of this book: that the ground rules of economic competition have shifted in important ways in recent years. Consequently, organisations need to adapt to these new rules if they are to survive and thrive in the new environment. In short, we find ourselves at a point where organisations will increasingly rely on knowledge for survival and competitive advantage. In the words of Charles Handy, 'focused intelligence — the ability to acquire knowledge and know-how — is the new source of wealth' (Handy, 1995:23). As such, these changes mean that finding the knowledge available within any organisation, and then putting that knowledge to work for the organisation, has become the key imperative of organisations at the start of this new century. This book offers a way of successfully doing that.

There is nothing more frightful than ignorance in action.
- JOHANN VON GOETHE

chapter two

Why You Need to Know about Knowledge Management

A little knowledge that acts is worth more than much knowledge that is idle.
– KAHLIL GIBRAN

What is Knowledge Management?

As bizarre as it may seem, given the number of column inches dedicated to the topic of 'knowledge management', there is precious little agreement about what the label actually means. Disagreements variously centre on the 'real' meaning of knowledge, on what managing it means, or even whether 'knowledge management' is an oxymoron. As a consequence, a significant number of people wonder whether this thing we call knowledge management should really be called something else. These are interesting questions (and, as ex-academics, we find ourselves needing to suppress our own pedantic urges here too) but they are not vital ones. In the real world, what matters is that knowledge management is about creating competitive advantage from the intellectual assets available to your organisation. In the introduction, with its talk of reinterpreting Francis Bacon and old IBM posters, we offered our own working definition. Two others we are particularly fond of are Stephen Denning's summary, that knowledge management is 'about connecting people who need to know with those who do know' (Denning, 2000:97), and our friend and colleague, Trevor Williamson's, notion that 'Knowledge is the stuff – management is how you get it moving.' The important point here is that you can call it what you want, and define it however you will, but the purpose remains the same – to work better through working smarter (see note 1, page 173). In the previous chapter, we captured this when we talked about the imperative for finding the knowledge available within the organisation, and then putting that knowledge to work for the organisation.

Of course, none of these sound-bite summaries really tells you very much about what knowledge management actually involves. In the introduction, we talked about how 'knowledge management' involved creating the systems that enable organisations to tap into the knowledge, experiences, and creativity of their staff, in order to improve the performance of those organisations. Stephen Denning, who would undoubtedly rather explain what was actually involved through an engaging anecdote, has this to say in a footnote in *The Springboard*:

> Knowledge management might be seen as comprising multiple dimensions, including knowledge strategy, communities of practice, help desks, knowledge bases, knowledge capture, knowledge storage, knowledge dissemination, knowledge taxonomies, quality assurance, authentication procedures, budget incentives, and knowledge measures. (Denning, 2000:114)

This book will have much more to say about the 'how' and 'what' of knowledge management, but in this chapter we want to talk a little bit about the 'why'. In the introduction, we emphasised how knowledge management is fundamentally purposive. The reason why organisations should grapple with the multiple dimensions enumerated by Denning is to help them achieve their strategic business goals – perhaps through achieving higher performance, being more efficient, or becoming more innovative. The e-newsletter *Knowledge Management News* defines it this way:

> 'Knowledge management is about connecting people to people and people to information to create competitive advantage.' (www.kmnews.com)

All of which leaves us with a working definition that signals the key elements of knowledge management:

> 'Knowledge Management' is about applying the knowledge assets available to your organisation to create competitive advantage.

We like this definition because it places the emphasis on both 'your organisation' and the creation of 'competitive advantage'. It tells us that knowledge becomes an asset only where it is active and useful. It becomes useful only in accordance with your organisation's broader strategic goals. This definition, therefore, makes it clear from the outset that knowledge management is about sharing knowledge, not for its own sake, but rather as a means for discovering ways that enable staff to carry out business processes faster, better, and at lower cost.

An important consequence of this definition is that knowledge management is not about managing *all* the knowledge that exists in your organisation – just that knowledge which helps achieve strategic goals. For instance, that Dave in Stores has a pet interest in the Treaty of Westphalia does not mean that you should dedicate space on the organisation's intranet to the issue of the development of religious tolerance in seventeenth-century Germany. This is not to say that your staff may not distil some important lessons or ideas from their pet interests (no matter how esoteric those interests are) that may be useful to the organisation. The point is that your knowledge management efforts need to focus on those lessons and ideas, and not the detail of the background which gave rise to them. The fact that some knowledge may actually prove counterproductive should be obvious to any organisation, but it is perhaps best illustrated here by a story told to us by the singularly ebullient Human Resources consultant Andrew Barney.

In October, a village of Indians asked their chief if the coming winter was going to be cold. Not really knowing the answer, the chief replied that the winter would be cold and that the members of the village should collect wood to be prepared. Being a good leader, he then went to a phone booth, called the National Weather Service and asked 'Is this winter going to be cold?' The man on the phone responded 'This winter is indeed going to be very cold.' So the chief went back to encourage his people to collect even more wood to be prepared. A week later he called the National Weather Service again, and asked again 'Is it going to be a very cold winter?' 'Yes,' the man replied, 'it's going to be a very cold winter.' The chief went back to his people and ordered them to go out and bring back every scrap of wood they could find. Two weeks later he called the National Weather Service again: 'Are you absolutely sure that this winter is going to be very cold?' 'Absolutely,' the man replied, 'the Indians are collecting wood like crazy.'

This story illustrates an important point about knowledge management. Neither knowledge nor knowledge sharing is a source of power per se: it is the *right* knowledge, shared at the *right* time, which confers power.

KNOWLEDGE MANAGEMENT

Why Should You Care?

Science leads to foresight, and foresight leads to action.
- AUGUST COMTE

Chapter one outlined how, in the new economy of the twenty-first century, knowledge has become the pre-eminent source of competitive advantage. As the macro-economic environment has changed, so have the imperatives for business organisation. In short, a new game is being played and new rules need to be followed. As organisations change to adapt to these new rules, knowledge management can help in two clear ways:

- as a response to the new rules of economic competition and business organisation (that is, as the best possible game plan); and
- as a tool for dealing with change.

This chapter will outline how knowledge management helps in both cases. First, though, we need to discuss why knowledge management warrants careful attention. And to do this we need to demonstrate the way that the conventional suite of planning tools used in most organisations undervalues (or even dismisses) the potential contribution that knowledge can make to organisational performance, or fails to adequately grapple with the content of that knowledge. The failure is apparent in the realm of economics, in accountancy, and even among many of the traditional approaches to business analysis and communication. In short, few companies have yet optimised the potential rewards of knowledge because they misunderstand what it is and what they need to do to leverage it. Let's have a look at three reasons why.

The Strange Economics of Knowledge

Conventional economic theory is premised on an assumption of diminishing returns. As a resource gets used up, its price increases. The higher price thus provides an impetus for buyers to conserve the resource and seek lower-cost alternatives (which, in turn, brings the price down again). Yet, as Robert Reich points out, intellectual capital grows more valuable as it is used (Reich, 1992:109). Unlike machinery, which eventually wears out and needs to be depreciated throughout its useful life, knowledge is a resource that increases the more it is used. Moreover, as Charles Handy explains, intellectual property (knowledge) simply does not behave like any other form of property. For instance, you cannot give it to someone else by simple decree (if you could, imagine how it easy it would have been to get through Economics 101!). Joseph Stiglitz, the chief economist at the World Bank, explains the differences like this:

The properties of dynamic processes driven by knowledge seem to ultimately derive from its scarcity-defying expansiveness or non-rivalrous aspect of knowledge. Once knowledge is discovered and made public, there is essentially zero-marginal cost to adding more users (in Rollo and Clarke, 2001:7).

Fortunately, for the non-economists among us, Thomas Stewart (1999:170-171) explains Stiglitz's point in a way that is much easier to grasp. Stewart notes:

- Knowledge can be used without being consumed. In the language of economics, it is 'non-subtractive'. This means that when you obtain some knowledge, you don't really take anything away from the person who shared it with you in the first place. Consider the difference between sharing a secret with somebody and sharing a bottle of wine with them. Or think about the simple example of an economics course at university. The professors share what they know, pass it on to their students, and still get to keep that knowledge to use another year.
- Because it is non-subtractive, a piece of knowledge can have multiple, simultaneous, 'owners'. In our university economics course example, successful lectures might mean that professors share their knowledge with 300 students at once. Indeed, the exam at the end of the course can be seen as a way of ensuring that those students have successfully retained that knowledge.
- Given that knowledge can have multiple owners, it can therefore be in more than one place at a time. In a conventional lecture, the knowledge being shared by the professor simultaneously passes into the notes of most of the students in the classroom. If the class was part of a distant education programme, those students might be separated by thousands of miles. Economists call physical assets 'rival assets' because users act as rivals for the specific use of those assets, but there is no such 'rivalry' with knowledge. Here you really can have your cake and eat it too.
- Knowledge has a cost structure that is different from that of traditional products. It is heavily front-loaded – that is, the cost of producing the first copy is disproportionately higher than that of producing subsequent copies. The more a product is made up of

knowledge (that is, the more intangible it is), the greater the difference between sunk and marginal costs. Consider the effort needed to make the original version of a piece of software, or a movie, or a book, and then consider how easy it then becomes to make subsequent copies. In our economics course example, the effort goes into writing the original version of the lecture. After that, copies of the notes can be produced for next to nothing (and, indeed, are sometimes provided free to students either in hard copy [as photocopies] or in electronic form [as e-mail files or PDFs hosted on web pages]).

o This heavily front-loaded cost structure means knowledge rarely has economies of scale. Generally, how much knowledge costs to produce is unaffected by how many people eventually use it. Authors have to put in as much effort for a book that is read by a handful of people as for one that dominates *The New York Times'* best-seller list. The professors in our economics course have to put as much effort into preparing a lecture that is attended by 30 students as into one attended by 300 students.

o The strangest thing about knowledge is that is unpredictable. There is no simple correlation between expenditure on knowledge and productivity gains. When you buy a physical asset (such as a building) there is always some kind of return, but when investing in knowledge assets there is always the risk that there will be no return at all. This unpredictability is also seen in the way two different companies that spend the same on knowledge may have vastly different results. Of all the students enrolling in our university course, some may use what they learn to create companies or build careers that pay substantial rewards; others may consider the course a waste of their time and bemoan the sacrifices they made to attend (such as catching up on their sleep, their friends, or their hobbies).

o The unpredictability of knowledge means that, ultimately, it has a value that cannot be assessed until it is already possessed. The irony here, as Stewart notes, is that a purchaser of knowledge cannot judge 'whether it is worth paying for a piece of information until he (sic) has it; but once he possesses it, he no longer needs to purchase it.' Our economics students need to sit in on a lecture to see if that lecture interests them, but – short of walking out halfway through – will have to sit to the end regardless of how interesting they find the class. In short, you don't know what you've got until you've got it.

○ Finally, knowledge blurs the distinction between products and services. To take a simple example, is Microsoft a service firm or an industrial one? Or what about Xerox, which sees itself as no longer simply selling photocopiers but providing business solutions? *Fortune* magazine grappled with this problem as long ago as 1993 before replacing the separate top 500 lists of industrial firms and service firms with one integrated list.

For reasons such as these, it should be clear the economic rules of a knowledge-based economy will be radically different from those we have inherited (and jury-rigged) from the old predictable processes of industrialisation. This is only reinforced when we consider how poorly conventional accounting tools grapple with valuing knowledge.

Accounting for Nothing?

If we think of the economy in terms of a game, then, in the same way that the discipline of economics provides the ground rules for that game, the practice of accounting provides a way of keeping score. Clearly, when the rules of the game change, new ways of keeping score are also likely to be needed. This is the challenge that traditional accountancy finds itself confronting with the rise of the knowledge-based economy: 'Traditional metrics don't force a company to consider how it is performing against new unorthodox competitors' (Hamel, 2000).

In the previous chapter, we talked about the obvious manifestations of this problem – companies that have market capitalisations many times their book value. Microsoft, as we saw, had a market capitalisation that was 99 times greater than the worth of the traditional assets described on the company's balance sheet. The Microsoft example is a good one because it reminds us that this is not simply an academic argument. What Microsoft has may be 'intangible' (and difficult to measure) but it certainly works – creating 21,000 millionaires among its employees in 1997 alone (Boyle, 2000:133).

The challenge that the rise of knowledge poses to accounting is a complex one. It involves a combination of conceptualising what counts as knowledge (which, as we will see in the next chapter, is just as problematic for non-accountants) and then ascribing a value to that knowledge. Given accountancy's dependence on counting, it is little surprise that a common response adopted is to simply focus on the tangible asset that stores the knowledge. Consequently, many accountants have seen intellectual capital in terms of the books, computer hard drives, and filing cabinets where that knowledge resides. Thus, the tendency has been to manage the forms rather than the substance of knowledge. The obvious problem, to use a wonderful phrase of Thomas Stewart, is that this is akin to a 'viticulturist paying more attention to the bottle than to the wine' (Stewart, 1999:56). Of course, it is easier to count the bottles than to assess the quality of the wine. So this is what traditional accounting practices do.

Except, as we saw with the Microsoft example, doing so has perverse effects. To take another example, and one close to our hearts, the real 'value' in our company, No Doubt Research, (beyond the experience and knowledge that resides in the heads of its principals) can be found in the many jotted notes, boxes of files, lecture notes, articles, reports, and ideas that we have recorded during the time that we have been involved in this kind of work (that is, all of our professional lives). And yet, none of those things show up in the company's asset register, nor in our own shareholder accounts. To put this another way, the real value of our company is invisible in the official company accounts.

THE DIVIDENDS FROM 'DUMBING DOWN'

With conventional accounting, a company that sells off 100 company cars before they are worn out has to record them as a loss. However, if that same company was to lay off 100 employees that it trained (and who have a considerable amount of know-how and ideas about the company), it doesn't have to record it anywhere. Indeed, such behaviour is often rewarded on the stock market, resulting in the directors receiving performance bonuses. Not only do the experiences and knowledge of the employees have no value in conventional measuring scales, but those scales may even actively reward companies that 'dumb down' (from Boyle, 2000:132).

It is for reasons like this that a number of practitioners and commentators are saying that the shift to the knowledge economy requires a fundamental shift in accounting practices. In the words of Judy Lewent, the CFO (Chief Financial Officer) of Merk and Co., 'in a knowledge-based company the accounting system doesn't capture anything, really' (quoted in Stewart, 1999:58). As we have intimated, this is because traditional accounting practices focus on tangible assets – the kinds of assets that determined worth in the old industrial economy – and inventory. What gets measured are the costs and not the value created. As a consequence, accounting provides companies with a great deal of information about financial and physical assets but precious little about their intellectual ones. To see what we mean, consider these simple questions:

- What is your organisation's expected Return on Investment (ROI) projected for the next 3 years?
- What is the net present value (NPV) of the fixed assets and on what basis are they being depreciated?
- Given the current level of shareholder funds, can the company afford to expand by acquisition financed by debt?

Now try these:

- What is the total value of the knowledge assets held by your organisation?
- Who are your key knowledge holders, and what is the value of the knowledge you would lose if they left to work for one of your competitors?
- Is the total pool of your human capital appreciating or depreciating in value, and by how much each year?

That most of you can readily answer (or readily find the answers to) the first three questions but are mystified by the last three demonstrates the extent to which accountancy is failing knowledge-intensive companies. The larger point here is that accountancy is yet to come to terms with the fact that the traditional relationship between current value and historical costs breaks down in the knowledge economy. We talked a little about this in chapter one when we introduced the idea of products becoming increasingly like professional services (in moving from congealed resources – a lot of material held together by a little knowledge – towards congealed knowledge – a little material held together by a lot of knowledge). As we said there, when you consider the cost of hiring a lawyer (or a knowledge management consultant!) for an hour then it is obvious that very little of the fee goes to pay for physical overheads. Most of it goes to pay for the knowledge held by the lawyer and their law firm. Except, even the professional services model is a misleading one. Professional services firms usually bill according to the time spent on a job – with time acting as a proxy for costs and precious little to do with the value of what is produced (Stewart, 1999:59). Why this is more than an interesting academic argument is because traditional accounting practices mask the value premium to be made from managing knowledge wisely. The 'brain gain', as Stewart calls it, does not show up on the balance sheet of the smart company.

To be fair to accountants, a number of them have attempted (and are attempting) to create relevant and useful metrics. For instance, Baruch Lev, from the New York University's Stern School of Business (see note 2, page 173), has created the 'Knowledge Capital Scoreboard'. This works on the concept of 'normalised earnings' – a measure which takes into account likely future earnings. Lev notes that one of the things that is 'fundamentally wrong with all of the other ways we have of accounting for earnings, including improvements such as EVA [Economic Value Added] [is that] they are all based on history. They are accounting in the past' (Webber, 2000:214). As one of our MBA students said to us once, 'Running your company using conventional accountancy techniques is like driving your car by looking in the rear-view mirror.' Although Baruch Lev is quickly making a name for himself as accountancy's best-known *agent provocateur*, the best-known attempt to account for intangible assets is the 'Navigator' developed for the Swedish insurance company, Skandia, by Leif Edvinsson and Karl Erik Sveiby. As (comparatively) early as 1995, Skandia was publishing an 'intellectual capital report' to augment its annual report and accounts (see note 3, page 173). The indicators the Navigator tracked ranged from the commonsensical – fund assets, income per employee, marketing expense per customer – to the unexpected – telephone accessibility, days spent visiting customers, information technology literacy, even laptop computers per employee. What we particularly like is the metaphor used by Skandia to explain the need for this new approach. They talk about the organisation as a 'tree', with the conventional measurement devices represented as the trunk, branches and leaves, noting that

> to assume that this is the entire tree because it represents everything immediately visible is obviously a mistake ... half the mass or more of that tree is underground in the root system. And whereas the flavor of the fruit and the color of the leaves provides evidence of how healthy that tree is right now, understanding what is going on in the roots is a far more effective way to learn how healthy that tree will be in years to come. (Edvinsson and Malone 1997:10)

What is pertinent here is how Skandia had to create their measures virtually in a vacuum. Edvinsson notes that 'there have always been occasional and temporary gaps between market perception and accounting reality [b]ut now that gap is turning into a chasm' (Edvinsson and Malone 1997:41). Equally, Karl Sveiby talks about how his entire working life started with a journey of 'unlearning'. He writes:

> My first job was as an auditor, unlearning what I had learnt about accounting in the university. It took two years 1972 to 1974 and I also learned that I was not fit to be an auditor. It took me six years as a manager in Unilever to unlearn the accountant experience. (www.sveiby.com.au/WhoamI.html)

There is no doubt in our minds that accountancy as a whole will change, but until it does (and until there is some agreement about how to value intangible intellectual assets), organisations are on their own. A former Chair of the US Financial Accounting Standards Board has gone as far as to describe the challenge of attempting to recognise intangible assets as 'insurmountable' (Ketz, 2001:2). Interestingly, the challenge that confronts the accounting profession is one that takes it back to its roots. As David Boyle points out (2000:38), there was a time when accountants were able to deal with this kind of uncountable world much better than they are now. In the early days of the American accountancy profession, accountants were urged to 'use figures as little as you can.' Boyle quotes James Anyon, 'the grand old man of American accounting,' who cautioned his colleagues: 'Remember your client doesn't like or want [figures], he wants brains. Think and act upon facts, truths, and principles and regard figures only as things to express these, and so proceeding you are likely to become a great accountant.'

In sum, the real reason why traditional economic theory and traditional accounting methods fail to adequately engage with the value of knowledge is that knowledge plays by different rules. Baruch Lev describes accounting as 'the last refuge of those who believe that things are assets and that ideas are expendable' (and has noted that the ways accountants have traditionally measured the economy are 'suddenly so out of date') (Boyle, 2000:132). David Boyle puts it like this: 'If football is the new rock 'n' roll, as they say, then information is the new money. Torrents of it flow across the world's computer screens every day … It's information, rather than money, that makes the world go round …' (2000:128).

Conceptualising, Analysing, and Communicating

All this talk about economics and accounting concentrates on the problems involved with *measuring* the value of knowledge. But the changing economy does more than challenge our traditional metrics;

it also challenges our traditional conceptual, analytical, and communication tools. In the words of Stephen Denning:

> The mechanistic analysis that we have applied ... has not always been much help to us. It doesn't fit the complexity, the mess, the jumble, the clutter, the chaos, the confusion, the living core of modern organizations. And it rarely succeeds in persuading organizations to change (2001:xvii).

Denning goes on to argue that traditional communication techniques work by engaging with the abstract dimension of our intelligence. This is that part of our intelligence that attempts analysis through detachment – that attempts to reduce problems to their constituent parts free of any superfluous details. The point of such analysis is that it strives to remain distant from the collective experiences, imagination, and emotions of those involved. And, although such an approach to analysis and communication certainly has its place in any organisation, coming to terms with the 'complexity, clutter, and chaos' of the modern workplace requires something more. For Denning, this is the use of 'narrative' techniques of analysis and communication. Here, stories are told that capture the key elements of a solution, thus communicating them through anecdote. Denning describes abstract reasoning as 'an uninhabited and uninviting place' whereas narrative techniques provide an approach that is 'pulsing, kicking, breathing, exciting – and alive' (2001, 63-5). James Gleick said it even better when he suggested that the abstract thinker 'invents his companions, as a naive Romeo imagined his Juliet.' By contrast, the narrative thinker's lovers 'sweat, complain, and fart' (Gleick 1987:124). In sum, narratives work because they provide 'the kind of plausibility, coherence, and reasonableness that enables people to make sense of immensely complex changes' (Denning, 2001:37). Interestingly, there is even an emerging field of 'narrative-based medicine', where doctors draw heavily on the stories patients tell to formulate their diagnoses and treatments.

Narrative techniques have another benefit too. As well as providing a way of grappling with (and communicating about) the 'complexity, clutter, and chaos' of the world, they also provide a way of engaging with their audience. A point we will repeatedly make in this book is that successful knowledge management is about reducing the amount of information staff are exposed to. One of the real challenges in knowledge management is the sorting, sifting, and reduction of knowledge. However, until systems are in place that achieve this, the limiting factor to your organisation's ability to learn is that the attention of your staff is a finite (and, to economists, a 'subtractive') resource. In the words of Thomas Davenport and John Beck, 'in this new economy information and knowledge are all in plentiful supply ... What's in short supply is human attention ...' (2001:2) and 'the most important function of attention isn't taking information in, but screening it out' (2001:58). Fortunately, storytelling (narrative) is one method of communication that commands our attention. Indeed, there is something profoundly atavistic about a story told well, and following such stories is both easy and largely unconscious. Contrast this with the effort needed to keep up with (or even stay awake during) the standard corporate PowerPoint presentation. Boyle notes that the audiences of these conventional presentations increasingly suffer from the MEGO syndrome – the 'my eyes glaze over' syndrome (Boyle, 2000:192). Denning argues that narratives are a superior way of analysing and communicating 'real world' problems because they are a 'better fit not only with the way our brains are made, but also with the underlying reality of the subject matter being discussed' (2001:116).

As researchers as well as knowledge management consultants, we are only too aware of how suspicious many managers are of qualitative data. The quickest way for us to get a client to start looking at us sideways is to mention the role that storytelling can play in helping staff understand and communicate complex problems. This reaction reminds us of Lord Kelvin's notion that:

> When you can measure what you are speaking about, and express it in numbers, you know something about it; but when you cannot measure it, when you cannot express it in numbers, your knowledge is of a meagre and unsatisfactory kind.

Mind you, Lord Kelvin also once asserted 'heavier-than-air flying machines are impossible,' so you need to be careful not to read too much into the great scientist's words! We are not suggesting that narratives *replace* traditional analytical techniques, merely that they supplement them where appropriate – in those kinds of situations Isadore Duncan might have meant when she said, 'If I could tell you what it meant, there would be no point in dancing it.'

To conclude this section, we have introduced the limitations of conventional economics, accounting, and analytical and communication tools to demonstrate (i) why organisations have traditionally failed to understand the value of focusing on knowledge, and (ii) why knowledge management has become such a popular topic (because it *does* attempt to grapple with those crucial aspects of the knowledge economy that conventional tools engage with so inadequately).

Where Does Knowledge Management Fit?

Nothing astonishes men so much as common sense and plain dealing.
– RALPH WALDO EMERSON

At the start of the last chapter, we outlined how it was clear to us that the ground rules of economic competition have shifted in important ways in recent years. In this chapter, we have introduced the idea that traditional business tools fail to come to terms with the new rules. It should be clear by now that organisations will increasingly rely on knowledge for survival and competitive advantage, and that knowledge management provides the key tool for achieving this.

In many regards, our enthusiasm for knowledge management means we often answer the question 'Where does knowledge management fit?' with the simple response 'Everywhere.' And although this is certainly true, it is of little use to those people who really want to know 'But where should I start?' Often, too, the real question is 'How can I sell knowledge management to the rest of the organisation?' Here we think there are two key areas to concentrate on:

○ improving organisational performance; and
○ managing organisational change.

Knowledge Management and Improving Organisational Performance

The key benefit of successful knowledge management is that it enables organisations to realise the value of the intellectual assets available to them. In this regard, knowledge management is very much about organisational performance. As we will see in the next chapter, the key dimension for distinguishing knowledge from information is *purpose*. Knowledge becomes knowledge, by definition, through providing an organisation with something useful (hence the idea of knowledge as 'packaged and useful intellectual assets'). The point here is that such assets can only ever become useful in accordance with an organisation's broader strategic goals. As we have seen, it is important to be clear that the 'knowledge' in knowledge management is not about knowledge for knowledge's sake. In this regard, initiating a knowledge management strategy is all about achieving competitive advantage. Although the ultimate goal of such a strategy is likely to be increased profitability, other common metrics of that advantage will include improved time-to-market performance, reduction of duplication, and promotion of intelligent collaboration.

WHAT ARE THE BENEFITS OF KNOWLEDGE MANAGEMENT?

The evidence for the benefits of knowledge management is unequivocal: organisations with strong knowledge management practices excel in every way. They are more likely to: be profitable; have a greater market share; be performing better than before they introduced knowledge management; be more flexible in dealing with change (and especially in responding to crises); have better workplace morale (and a greater sense of organisational coherence); and be more likely to develop innovative products than organisations without such practices (Scherer, 2001). Other benefits include: superior strategic decision-making ability; closer relationships with customers and suppliers; improved operational performance; a better ability to differentiate products and services; and a superior strategic competitive advantage.

The Australian Standards Authority provides the following list of ways a knowledge management strategy can tailor particular kinds of benefits to the core business of an organisation (all Rollo and Clarke, 2001:13):

- Industries based on innovation can use knowledge management to accelerate the process of research and development, and to manage intellectual property.
- Companies offering professional services can use knowledge management to enhance (by broadening or deepening) their expertise.
- Industries founded on the creation of intangibles (such as entertainment or publishing) can employ knowledge management to develop creative skills and networks, and to protect intellectual capital.
- Industries relying on relationships (such as retail) can use knowledge management to enhance customer service and offer greater product and service depth and quality.
- Companies dependent on the value of brands (such as fashion) can use knowledge management to improve their market intelligence.

○ Companies requiring good coordination of complex activities (such as manufacturing) can use knowledge management to increase control.

Each of these purposes will require different strategic knowledge management approaches, and underscores the central point of this book – that there is no simple recipe for successful knowledge management (see chapter six). Examples of different strategies in action, and proof that successful knowledge management can deliver the goals outlined above, are provided by a number of international cases. For those who are interested, we suggest a closer examination of:

Sector	Company	Web Address
Aerospace	Boeing	www.boeing.com
Automotive	Ford	www.ford.com
Banking	Canadian Imperial Bank of Commerce	www.cbic.com
Energy	BP Amoco PLC	www.bpamoco.com
	Shell Oil Company	www.shell.com
Information Technology	Hewlett-Packard	www.hp.com
	Xerox Corporation	www.xerox.com
	Microsoft	www.microsoft.com
Insurance	Skandia Insurance	www.skandia.com
Military	US Army	www.army.mil
Pharmaceuticals	Pfizer Inc.	www.pfizer.com
Professional Services	Ernst and Young	www.ey.com
	KPMG Consulting	www.kpmg.com
Technology	Texas Instruments	www.ti.com

The final point that needs to be made in this brief overview is that, although it is undoubtedly the case that knowledge management does need to be linked to (and integrated with) the broader organisational performance strategy, this should not prevent organisations from embarking on a knowledge management project as a catalyst for reinventing that strategy.

A NEW ZEALAND PERSPECTIVE: MANAGING THE 'KNOWLEDGE WAVE'

In 2001, there was much publicity about 'Catching the Knowledge Wave' in New Zealand. This was a joint initiative by the New Zealand Government in partnership with the University of Auckland, supported by business and community groups. The goal was 'to find practical ways to secure New Zealand's long-term future as a smarter, more prosperous and successful country' (www.knowledgewave.org.nz). Watching the initiative unfold (and culminate in a major conference in August 2001), we were struck by how the philosophy of knowledge management could work at a national level as readily as at an organisational one. As we will see in chapter five, organisations can increase their knowledge stocks when they either make more use of what their people already know, or when more people know more things that are useful to the organisation. Clearly, these ideas hold as well for New Zealand as a whole as they do for any New Zealand organisation. Moreover, the discipline of knowledge management offers a number of useful suggestions about how to maximise the knowledge available in each case, thus suggesting that it might be as useful for social policy planners as corporate strategic ones.

Knowledge Management and Managing Organisational Change

Another way to introduce knowledge management is as a mechanism for helping manage organisational change initiatives. For instance, and most immediately obviously, knowledge management processes provide a way that organisations can identify where their key intellectual assets reside, thus supporting the selection of staff to be out-placed or retained. For those staff who are being out-placed, knowledge management processes provide a way of capturing a measure of the relevant intellectual assets they have developed while with the organisation (and, equally, by having those staff reflect on what they know, helping them prepare to enter the labour market). At a broader level, knowledge management supports organisational change initiatives by providing a mechanism that helps seed (and nurture) the new organisational culture. These benefits are particularly noticeable in terms of the cross-functional exposure and awareness staff experience following the change. Moreover, the introduction of a knowledge management project can itself become the catalyst for a broader organisational change initiative (precisely because realising successful knowledge management is about cultural change). In Trevor Williamson's memorable phrase, 'Change leaders need to be knowledge leaders.' Finally, the incremental and iterative nature of the knowledge management process means that organisations have the option of a soft entry into change initiatives by pursuing change benefits for a small initial investment.

Knowledge Management: More than Just Another Fad?

*Everything has been thought of before,
but the problem is to think of it again.*
– JOHANN GOETHE

Another question we are frequently asked is 'How do we know that knowledge management is not just another fad?' We usually answer this question by saying that 'Knowledge Management' (with a capital K and M) may well prove to be a fad, but the principles of managing knowledge (with a small m and k) surely are not. We say this because, although the notion of knowledge management as an integrated subject is a new phenomenon, many of its components are not. Indeed, good managers are likely to have been unconscious knowledge managers their entire careers. Indeed, the logic of knowledge management can be traced through many of the management theory fads of the 1980s and 1990s. To put this another way, 'knowledge is not new, but recognising it as a corporate asset is' (Davenport and Prusak, 1998:12). What has changed in recent years is that many organisations have started to realise that they require 'more than a casual (or even unconscious) approach to corporate knowledge if they are to succeed in today's and tomorrow's economies' (Davenport and Prusak, 1998:ix).

Our friend and colleague Ian Ris makes the point that thinking in terms of 'fads' can mask many of the real benefits that knowledge management offers, because fads fade from conscious view precisely when their principles and practices become normalised into daily routines. For instance, although the Total Quality Management (TQM) 'fad' is now as trendy as big hair and designer stubble, few organisations fail to take quality issues seriously. Indeed, there is little need to argue for the value of quality because it has become inculcated in the common sense of most organisations. This book argues that the development of knowledge management will follow a similar path, moving from knowledge management as a project to knowledge management as an integral part of workplace culture (see chapters six and seven).

That said, we are also big fans of the fad of Knowledge Management (with the capital K and M) because its popularity provides organisations with an imperative to act. It is one thing to talk about the value of knowledge and its contribution to competitive advantage but it is quite another to amend your organisational culture to seriously engage with that knowledge. In a knowledge economy where applied knowledge is *the* source of competitive advantage, it is obvious that organisations need to tap into, and apply, the knowledge of their staff. This is what knowledge management really provides — ways to get the useful knowledge out of the heads of your staff and into the workplace where it can do some good.

chapter three

Knowledge Management 101

Doubt may be an uncomfortable position but certainty is a ridiculous one.
– VOLTAIRE

Why Definitions Are Important

This chapter outlines the basic concepts used in any discussion about knowledge management. It introduces such issues as the differences between knowledge, information, and data; the meaning of intellectual capital; and the various kinds of intellectual capital available to your organisation. If you are already comfortable with these ideas, it may pay to skip this chapter and move on to chapter four.

In the previous chapter, we introduced our definition of knowledge management and noted how there were almost as many such definitions as there are people writing about the subject. The same problem pervades the ideas we are going to introduce in this chapter, where the disagreements are, if anything, even more apparent. It is certainly the case, for instance, that people have been arguing over questions such as 'What is knowledge?' for almost as long as they have been getting together in civilisations. One approach might be to argue that the distinctions that determine definitions are esoteric constructs best left to philosophers, and best entirely avoided by practitioners. As with the contested notion of knowledge management itself, we have some sympathy with those who essentially respond to any question of definitions with the question 'Does it really matter?' However, we think some definitions *do* matter because we believe it has been a failure to be clear about these differences that has led to so many experiences of failure and false starts with knowledge management in the past.

For instance, it is partially because many people have seen the new economy as being an information economy that they are such fervent believers that information technologies offer the appropriate solution. We would argue that it is precisely because it is a *knowledge* economy that they can't (see chapter four). As Charles Jonscher notes, if you're not clear about your definitions, then 'it is easy to be misled into thinking that a tool which produces data is also producing knowledge' (2000:195).

Data, Information, and Knowledge

One of the problems with the label 'knowledge management' is that it immediately begs questions about 'What is knowledge?' and 'How do you manage it?' Later chapters will deal with the second question, but here we want to try and grapple with the first. As noted above, the question 'What is knowledge?' is the kind of epistemological question that has preoccupied philosophers for as long as we have had philosophy. In many regards, it is easier to talk about what we *don't* mean when we talk about knowledge.

What we *can* say about knowledge is that it is distinct from both data and information (concepts that are also critical to knowledge management). Data, information, and knowledge are not interchangeable concepts. Indeed, understanding what these three things are and how you get from one to another is 'essential to doing knowledge work successfully' (Davenport and Prusak, 1998:1). Furthermore, as the world becomes more comprehensively wired, 'we will need more than ever to understand the difference between data, information, and knowledge' (Jonscher, 2000:252).

A useful way to think of these three concepts is as a hierarchy (with data at the bottom and knowledge at the top).

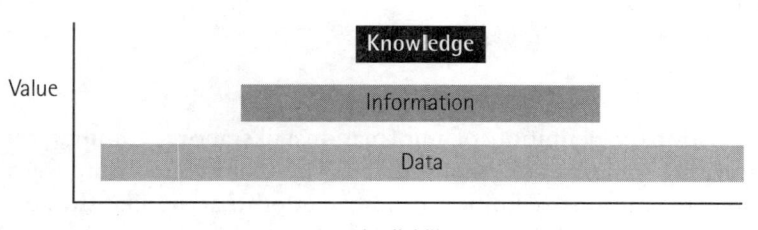

Data
The airplane rides are three dollars. Cash.
– RICHARD BACH

Look in a dictionary and you will be told that 'data' is the plural of 'datum', and that a 'datum' is 'something given or admitted especially as a basis for reasoning or inference' or 'something used as a basis for calculating or measuring' (from *The Merriam-Webster Collegiate Dictionary* at http://www.m-w.com). Your dictionary may also tell you that the words can be traced back to the Latin word for 'given' (as in, it is a given that dictionaries tell you much more information than you ever need to know). Bill Bryson argues that 'the sense of the word [should] be confined to the idea of raw, uncollated bits of information, the sort of stuff churned out by computers, and not used as a simple synonym for "facts" or "reports" or "information"' (Bryson, 1987:53).

Bryson's idea is right on the money, but for the sake of brevity we tend to use Thomas Davenport and Larry Prusak's notion that data are 'discrete, objective, facts about events' (1998:2). In organisations, data represent 'structured records of transactions' (*Ibid.*) The important point here is that **there is no inherent meaning in data**. Data may be the raw material of decision making, but they cannot, alone, tell you what to do. Davenport and Prusak use the example of a customer buying some petrol for her car: the data collected will record how many litres she bought, when she bought them, how much she paid, and how she paid. But the data cannot tell us anything about why she went to that petrol station and not another, nor how happy she was with the service, nor whether she is likely to go back to purchase more petrol in the future. All organisations need data, and some organisations are entirely reliant on them. However, more data are not always better. Too many data make it hard to distinguish the useful data from the noise.

Information
All truths are only half truths.
- ALFRED NORTH WHITEHEAD

The dictionary definition of information talks about 'communication concerning some fact or circumstance'. The word comes from the verb 'to inform' and one definition of information that we like stresses 'the act of informing'. In this regard, information is different from data because it has meaning. Indeed, this is where the hierarchy represented above begins to make some sense, because we can conceptualise 'information' as simply **'data invested with meaning'** (that is, information = data + meaning). Peter Drucker makes the same point by noting that information is 'data endowed with relevance and purpose.' Charles Jonscher is even more precise when he describes information as 'data interpreted by the person who is being informed' (Jonscher, 2000:36).

Information, then, can be thought of as a message that is intended to have an impact on the receiver. It adds meaning to data in a number of ways, with some of the most common ones being through

- contextualisation (why were the data gathered in the first place?),
- categorisation (what are the key components of the data?),
- calculation (for instance, through statistical summaries),
- correction (involving the discovery and removal of errors), and
- condensation (with the main points summarised in a more concise form).

Although this list is far from comprehensive, it is useful because it draws our attention to the fact that although computers can do many of these transformations, they are incapable of doing them all. For instance, putting the data into context is something only people can do. As we will see, it is this 'social construction' element of information that has important consequences for knowledge management.

Knowledge
Where is the knowledge we have lost in information?
– T S ELIOT

When we first started No Doubt Research (back in 1998) we paraphrased T S Eliot's words for the new company's strap line. The back of our business cards (and our brochures, website, T-shirts, etc.) reproduced the line 'Knowledge is more than information.' We even intended framing the poem this line came from, *The Rock*, and putting it on our office wall (see note 4, page 173). We think this line beautifully encapsulates the idea that knowledge is broader, deeper, and more useful than information. It also underscores the value of the hierarchy outlined above because, just as information is *data* distilled and interpreted, knowledge is *information* distilled and interpreted. In the same way that we add meaning to data to transform it into information, **we add purpose to information to transform it into knowledge** (that is, knowledge = information + purpose).

Philosophers have debated the origin, nature, methods and limits of knowledge (in the branch of philosophy known as epistemology) for millennia. Although knowledge may remain a philosophically slippery concept, this does not mean that we have any trouble recognising it when we see it. The problem may not be in understanding what it is but in the act of formulating definitions in general. One of the most famous philosophers of the twentieth century, Ludwig Wittgenstein, illustrated this general problem with definitions by talking about the concept of a 'game'. Wittgenstein argued that it was not possible to establish the necessary and sufficient conditions for an activity to be judged a game because 'when one tries, one invariably finds an activity that one's definition includes but that one would not want to count as a game, or an activity that the definition excludes but that one would want to count as a game' (quoted in Chalmers, 1982:93). We think it is the same with defining knowledge: explicit definitions either include or exclude activities that none of us would want to count. But, just as Wittgenstein's difficulty with defining 'game' does not mean we cannot use that term legitimately, the failure to precisely define 'knowledge' does not make that term untenable either.

Davenport and Prusak (1998:6–7) suggest some of the components that we might all agree contribute to 'knowledge':

- *Experience:* knowledge develops over time. This means experience provides a historical perspective from which to view and understand new situations and events.
- *Practical utility:* knowledge means being able to distinguish what 'should' work from what really does. It is where 'the rubber meets the road.' It is the difference between what is taught in business schools and what really happens in the business world.
- *Speed:* the knowledgeable are able to recognise patterns and provide short cuts to solutions rather than build them from scratch every time. As a result, knowledge offers supercharged problem-solving.
- *Complexity:* knowledge is about dealing with complexity. This means the knowledgeable are comfortable with the ambiguity of real-world situations. By denying complexity, those without knowledge offer simple solutions that invariably fail.
- *Evolution:* because the key to knowledge is knowing what you don't know, the knowledgeable are also able to refine their knowledge through further experience, study, and learning. Knowledge either examines itself and evolves or it is dogma.

Some of the processes used to transform information into knowledge include:

- comparisons (How does this compare with what else we know?)
- consequences (What does this information suggest we should do?)

○ connections (How does this relate to others?)
○ conversation (What do other people think of this information?)

Finally, knowledge involves a dimension of 'resolution' and of 'action'. It involves resolution in the sense that, although you may have conflicting information, it is unusual for someone to say they have conflicting knowledge. Equally, someone might say 'I have the information but I don't understand it', but you would think it bizarre if they said 'I have that knowledge but I don't understand it' (Brown and Duguid, 2000:120). It involves action because the role of 'purpose' is so important in the creation of knowledge. In other words, 'knowledge can and should be evaluated by the decisions and actions to which it leads' (Davenport and Prusak, 1998:6).

This brief discussion about the differences between data, information, and knowledge leaves us with a taxonomy that looks like this:

From Data to Knowledge

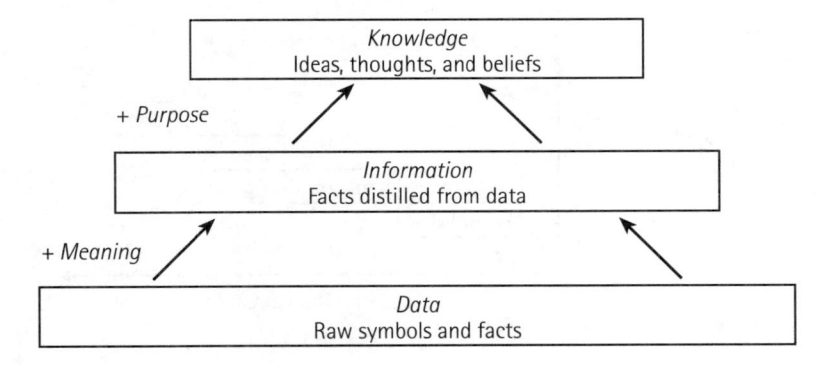

```
                    ┌─────────────────────────────────┐
                    │         Knowledge               │
                    │  Ideas, thoughts, and beliefs   │
                    └─────────────────────────────────┘
                              ↗           ↖
        + Purpose
                    ┌─────────────────────────────────┐
                    │         Information             │
                    │    Facts distilled from data    │
                    └─────────────────────────────────┘
                              ↗           ↖
        + Meaning
                    ┌─────────────────────────────────┐
                    │            Data                 │
                    │     Raw symbols and facts       │
                    └─────────────────────────────────┘
```

Other Perspectives on 'Knowledge'

Another approach to defining knowledge is to break it down into four operational levels. This is the approach taken by James Quinn, Philip Anderson, and Sydney Finkelstein (1998). Although they apply it specifically to the knowledge of professional staff (see note 5, page 173) the model can hold across all types of knowledge.

○ 'Know what': also called 'cognitive knowledge', this is the essential disciplinary knowledge achieved through training, studies, and

formal qualifications. It is vital for any enterprise but is 'usually far from sufficient for commercial success' (Quinn et al., 1998:183).
- 'Know how': this is the level of practical application. It is where the learning achieved at the 'know what' phase is translated into doing. This is also the area where most professional knowledge adds value in an organisation through the ability to translate theoretical knowledge into effective execution.
- 'Know why': also called 'systems understanding', this is the 'deep knowledge of the web of cause-and-effect relationships underlying a discipline' (Quinn et al., 1998:183). This allows professionals to move beyond the execution of tasks to solve larger and more complex problems and create new solutions to new problems.
- 'Care why': although much learning stops at the 'know why' stage, there is a further stage of self-motivated creativity. This is where radical innovation can occur through imaginative leaps and lateral thinking.

These four stages are most clearly demonstrated by the following diagram:

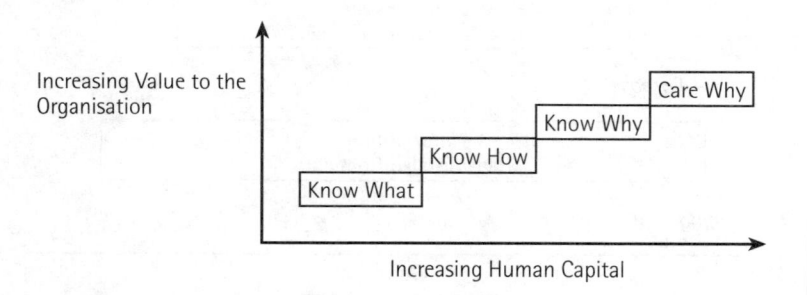

Increasing Value to the Organisation

Know What — Know How — Know Why — Care Why

Increasing Human Capital

Consider an example close to our hearts – teaching students how to conduct social and market research. We can provide our students with an overview of what is involved in running, say, focus groups, in a couple of short lessons. Armed with the notes from those lessons, the textbook, and a checklist or two (the sort of thing we would undoubtedly provide as a handout), the students would thus have achieved the 'know what' of focus groups. After they have been out into the 'real world' and tried to run a focus group or two, made the same mistakes all novices do, and talked to some more experienced colleagues, the students – eventually – would develop the 'know how' of focus groups. However, it takes many years of practice (and study) to understand why focus groups work the way they do, and when it's appropriate to break the rules or at least mix them up a little. Indeed, for some research problems it might even pay to mix the qualitative research logic of focus groups with a quantitative research design. Knowing when to do those sorts of things (solving real world research problems 'on your feet' by adapting the rules of various research methods) is the 'know why' phase (see note 6, page 173).

Quinn and his colleagues go on to suggest that the first three levels of knowledge can also exist as structural capital (see below) but the fourth level ('care why') is uniquely the preserve of staff. However, they also note that for this knowledge to emerge, organisations need to develop cultures that encourage creativity. We consider this issue in chapters five and seven.

LET THEM EAT ... DATA

Charles Jonscher (2000:252) has a neat way of distinguishing data, information, and knowledge:

> the difference between data and knowledge is like the difference between raw food and the nourishment we obtain by eating it. An intermediate step, like information, is the meal we prepare from the raw ingredients and serve on the plate. Data's role in the quest for knowledge, like raw food's role in the quest for nourishment, is the starting point: the vegetables, the grains, and the livestock in the fields. We then make it into a meal, selecting the raw foodstuffs according to our needs and processing them for taste and digestibility. The process may be light, as in cleansing a salad or squeezing a fruit juice, or heavy, as in making milk into butter or meat into stew. Then we eat the prepared food to obtain nourishment: energy to live and chemicals to renew and grow our bodily cells. Knowledge is like the nourishment we receive after taking in and digesting the meal.

But What About Wisdom?

We cannot be taught wisdom, we have to discover it for ourselves by a journey which no-one can undertake for us.
- MARCEL PROUST

The one problem with any hierarchy of knowledge is that it begs an obvious question about what lies beyond knowledge. Where do you go to next? We have talked about knowledge as *information with purpose* and stressed that knowledge involves being able to *act*. But what about knowing when to act and when to sit still? In that famous phrase of Benjamin Disraeli's, 'next to knowing when to seize an opportunity, the most important thing in life is knowing when to forego an advantage.' What term can we use to describe the combination of knowledge and judgement? Some people have suggested that the logical step up on the hierarchy would be to 'wisdom'. Indeed, the T S Eliot poem that our company likes so much actually reads:

> Where is the knowledge we have lost in information?
> Where is the wisdom we have lost in knowledge?

Although we are distinctly uncomfortable talking about notions as lofty as 'wisdom' – we have enough trouble with 'knowledge' – it does capture something about the whole purpose of knowledge management. Indeed, the 'care why' phase in the taxonomy developed by Quinn and his colleagues (above) does already start to look pretty close to conventional definitions of wisdom. When we think of wisdom, we think of ideas like astuteness, perception, and judiciousness. Consequently, there might be a good case to argue that knowledge management is, really, interested in the creation and application of *wisdom*. Perhaps what we are all really interested in, ultimately, should be called Wisdom Management? Still, we should all be glad that it's not.

The relationship between data, information, knowledge, and wisdom is an important (albeit controversial and contested) one. The *New Hamlyn Encyclopedic World Dictionary* (London, 1988) – perhaps the best dictionary either of us has ever actually owned (gifts of the twenty-volume Oxford English Dictionary will be gleefully accepted by the authors!) – even dedicates a footnote to its definition of 'information' that reads:

> INFORMATION, KNOWLEDGE, and WISDOM are terms for human acquirements through reading, study, and practical experience. INFORMATION applies to facts told, read, communicated, which may be unorganized or even unrelated: *to pick up useful information*. KNOWLEDGE is an organized body of information, or the comprehension and understanding consequent on having acquired and organized a body of facts: *a knowledge of chemistry*. WISDOM is a knowledge of people, life, and conduct, with the facts so thoroughly assimilated as to have produced sagacity, judgement, and insight: *to use wisdom in handling people* (1988:850).

IN A SPIN OVER DEFINITIONS

The distinctions between data, information, knowledge, and wisdom are perhaps easy to understand through the use of an example. One of us (Carl) likes to fly light aeroplanes for light relief whenever he can find the time, and uses the example of 'spinning' his aeroplane to demonstrate the differences between these key knowledge management concepts. Once common, spinning-related accidents are much less of a problem for recreational pilots today thanks to the way that aeroplanes have developed. However, they can still be a problem during poorly executed aerobatics. How many pilots successfully recover from unintentional spins? How many pilots actually still die in spinning-related accidents? Fortunately, many fewer than did once upon a time. The important point for our purposes is that those numbers are merely *data*. If you ask to incorporate a lesson on spinning into your pilot training, then your instructor will provide you with some material to read for homework. Beyond what the flying school provides, there are a number of books on how to get out of a spin alive. Indeed, your flying instructor will likely provide a lesson on the ground about the dynamics of spinning. But all this material is merely *information*. And it is precisely because this is information and not knowledge that flying schools don't simply say 'Read this, do this, and then go and give it a try on your own'. Needless to say, no amount of reading about spins prepares you for what they feel like or for how fast the plane falls out of the sky.

> **The thing which stands out most ... is how my instructor's caution that 'the aeroplane will be moving around all three axes in a fully developed spin, and you might find that a little disorienting' seemed entirely inadequate compared to the experience of finding myself wondering where the horizon went (Davidson, 2000).**

Developing the *knowledge* of what happens in a spin (for example, that some planes actually momentarily increase their rate of rotation once you put anti-spin control inputs in), of what one looks and feels like, requires a combination of information and experience. To begin with, recovering from a spin is all about numbers (airspeed, engine rpm, etc.) and rote-learned steps (1. Throttle closed; 2. Opposite rudder to arrest the yaw; 3. Pause; 4. Stick forward to break the stall; etc.), but, in time, it becomes all about how the aeroplane feels and sounds (and even, believe it or not, how it smells). Finally, having become knowledgeable about spins, most pilots develop the *wisdom* to never go near one. Wisdom, though, is also all about judgement. In the case of spinning, it involves being able to distinguish between the onset of an unintentional spin and how to get into one as quickly as possible during your aerobatic routine. It turns out that spins are tremendous fun once you have mastered them, and you are clear about when it's okay to play with one.

We have spent some time on this taxonomy because we believe the various categories of data, information, knowledge (and even wisdom) play very different roles in successful knowledge management. As a participant in one of our courses on knowledge management put it, 'So, in effect, successful knowledge management is about having the wisdom to tell knowledge and information apart.'

The problem with the taxonomy, however, is that it suggests that the various categories are discrete and fixed. And although they may be for an individual, the definitions become much more slippery when we are describing an organisation or a group of people. Here we soon discover that what is knowledge to one person may be only information or data to another. Equally, what one person sees as a jumble of meaningless data may be the core of another person's knowledge base. For organisations, there is an important lesson in the definition of knowledge as a combination of information and purpose (and of information as combining data and meaning). When staff become overloaded with either knowledge or information, what is lost is purpose and meaning. Knowledge can easily become devalued into information, and information can deteriorate into data. If staff cannot distinguish the key messages from the trivial ones, then those messages are wasted. This happened at Andersen Consulting, which established a complex intranet called the Knowledge Xchange. As one manager there put it: 'We've got so much knowledge in our Knowledge Xchange repository that our consultants can no longer make sense of it ... for many of them it has become data' (quoted in Davenport and Prusak, 1998:7).

What is Intellectual Capital?

They copied all they could follow but they couldn't copy my mind, and I left 'em sweating and stealing a year and a half behind.
— RUDYARD KIPING

Another way to think about the data–information–knowledge taxonomy is via the notion of intellectual capital. For individuals, intellectual capital can be thought of as the sum of their imagination, intelligence, and ideas. But what about organisations? Thomas Stewart, whose book *Intellectual Capital* broke a great deal of ground for knowledge management in this regard, describes it as

- the sum of everything everybody in a company knows that gives it a competitive advantage (Stewart, 1999:xix);
- intellectual material – knowledge, information, intellectual property, experience – that can be put to use to create wealth (Stewart, 1999:xx); and
- packaged useful knowledge (Stewart, 1999:67).

The notion of 'intellectual capital' is a useful one because it identifies the common sources of data, information, and knowledge available to any organisation. These are:

- the talents of your people. This is the organisation's **human capital**, the collected knowledge and brainpower of its employees. '[I]t is the source of innovation and renewal, whether from brainstorms in a lab or new leads in a sales rep's little black book.' (Stewart, 1999:76)
- the knowledge captured in your systems and processes. This is the organisation's **structural capital**. Think of it as those structures that enable human capital to be captured and reused. This includes anything that turns individual know-how into knowledge for the organisation.
- the character of your relationships with your customers and suppliers. This is your organisation's **customer/supplier** capital. It is about the depth, width, and strength of those relationships (and, hence, the likelihood that those people will continue to do business with you).

Note that 'intellectual capital' is not created by having discrete amounts of each of these things – instead it comes from the interplay of all three (structural capital augments the value of human capital, leading to an increase in customer/supplier capital).

Sources of Intellectual Capital

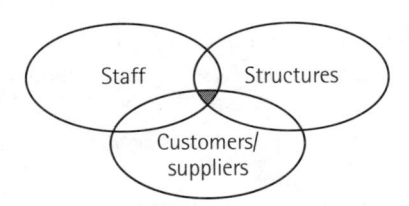

A Note About Intellectual Property: 'Intellectual capital' should not be confused with 'intellectual property'. Intellectual property is that subset of intellectual capital that can be protected by law – such as anything you can copyright or patent (works, ideas, discoveries, inventions, etc.). To qualify as intellectual property, your intellectual capital has to be unique, novel, and non-obvious (and, of course, it has to have some value, or potential value, in the marketplace). This might include unique

- names or descriptors;
- business methods;
- industrial processes;
- chemical formulae;
- computer program processes; or
- presentations, process manuals, handbooks, and so on.

The distinction between intellectual 'capital' and 'property' is an important one from a knowledge management perspective because knowledge does not have to be new to be useful, simply new to the organisation. To say this another way, it doesn't need to be intellectual property to act as intellectual capital. Originality is much less important than usefulness. This means that organisations need to work to overcome the 'Not Invented Here' (NIH) phenomenon. The Spanish proverb that says 'well stolen is half done' captures the idea. As we will see, those organisations that have recognised this have introduced awards for the best ideas 'borrowed' from elsewhere. Texas Instruments now has a 'Not Invented Here, But I Did it Anyway' award for the best idea stolen from within or without the company (Davenport and Prusak, 1998:53).

Human Capital
There is an old Maori proverb that says:
Pātai mai he aha te mea nui o te ao
Ka whakahoki au
He tāngata, he tāngata, he tāngata.

Which translates into English as:
Ask me what is the most important thing in the world
And I will reply
It is people, it is people, it is people.

From a knowledge management perspective, the people available to any organisation are seen as that organisation's human capital. In general, these people have two distinct kinds of knowledge: there is the kind of knowledge that can be easily articulated and shared with others (such as the recipe your grandmother used to bake her scones) and then there are those things you know but don't know how to articulate (such as how your grandmother knew exactly when to stop mixing the ingredients together to ensure the sweetest scones imaginable). The first kind of knowledge – the kind that is easy to articulate and share with others – is known as **explicit knowledge**. The second kind, the kind you know but don't know how to express, is known as **tacit knowledge**.

Tacit Knowledge

Most often associated with the work of the philosopher Michael Polanyi (1958), the distinction between tacit and explicit knowledge demonstrates that we can know more than we can tell or explain to others. Much of our knowledge is thus tacit – unable to be communicated in words or symbols. This means that people often know far more than they realise. Over the years that they work in a job they develop 'huge repertoires of skills, information, and ways of working that they have internalized to the point of obviousness' (Stewart, 1999:72). A beautiful passage in George Dawson's book, *Life Is So Good*, captures this idea when he talks about his job in the Oaks Farm Dairy factory: 'I kept things running. They counted on me. If I didn't come to work there wasn't no-one to replace me. I always set the gauges right [and] I did that without reading' (2000:223).

Similarly, John Seely Brown and Paul Duguid tell a story about a typesetter working on a Greek text at the Oxford University Press who noticed a mistake in the text. As the typesetter couldn't actually read Greek, his colleagues and then his supervisor dismissed his claim. But the typesetter insisted, and eventually an editor came down to the compositing room. She too dismissed the typesetter's claim, until she looked a little more closely and saw that indeed there was a mistake. When she asked him how he knew it was wrong, he said that he had been hand setting Greek texts for most of his professional life and he was sure that he had never picked out the two letters in that order before (2000:80).

The thing about tacit knowledge is that it deals with knowledge that has become so thoroughly embedded that the holders no longer think about what they're doing but simply do it. Watch someone perform some highly skilled activity they are good at (be it in the workplace, on the sports field, in the kitchen, or wherever) and then ask them afterwards why they did it that way. We bet that the most common answer you hear will be along the lines of 'It's common sense,' or 'I just do.' This is the area of study known as 'naturalistic decision making'. In aviation, for instance, naturalistic decision making is being used to explain why experienced pilots seem to make the right choices, most of the time, when faced with a tricky situation (Ewing, 2001:33). When faced with a complex decision, people use strategies that draw on their experiences and judgements. Of course, naturalistic decision making sounds an awful lot like 'gut feel' or 'manager's intuition', and the whole point of this field of study is to understand how those decisions get made so the processes can be taught to less-experienced managers (and pilots).

In most business situations, especially in the professions, the bulk of an individual's valuable and useful knowledge is tacit rather than explicit. Consequently, as we will see in chapter six, a key element of knowledge management is finding ways to communicate this kind of tacit knowledge, of turning tacit knowledge into explicit knowledge. Recognising the value of tacit knowledge leads to recognising the value of the people who work for any organisation. In the words of David Boyle: 'In the end ... the difference comes down to people, their instincts and their intuitions' (2000:151).

Talking about what tacit knowledge is takes us into some very interesting (and mysterious) places. For instance, Jaron Lanier, one of the pioneers of virtual reality, talks about how much tacit knowledge is required simply to communicate with another person. He writes:

> You can believe that a conversation between two people consists of objectifiable pieces of information that are transmitted from one to the other and decoded by algorithms, or that meaning is something ... that no-one has yet been able to find a method of reducing. Two people communicating with each other is an extraordinary phenomenon that has so far defied all attempts to capture it (in Jonscher, 2000:251).

In chapter six, we'll talk about how you can create mechanisms to facilitate the sharing of tacit knowledge.

TACIT KNOWLEDGE IN ACTION

There is a practical exercise we use in our courses about knowledge management that illustrates the difference between tacit and explicit knowledge. It involves dividing the course into two groups and having one group write a set of easy-to-follow instructions about how to ride a bicycle for someone who has never ridden before –

and who will have to learn to do so only from their written instructions. We then get them to give their instructions to the other group, who have to assess the quality and comprehensiveness of those instructions. We prompt this second group by asking questions such as 'What have these instructions left out?' and 'What knowledge have they taken for granted?' The exercise can be extended to any common skill – such as how to swim, or even how to stand on your head. To see how complex these common skills really are (or, to put this another way, to realise how much tacit knowledge is required to make them work), try the exercise for yourself. And then find some seemingly simple taken-for-granted skill in your organisation and get your staff to do the same.

Explicit Knowledge

Explicit knowledge is the easy part of human capital. It describes those things that we can write down (and, hence, easily share with others). This means it is easy to store and track. Your grandmother's recipe for scones is an obvious example, but so is everything in your organisation that can legitimately be reduced to a step-by-step guide. One of our favourite examples is the little screen on the photocopier in our office that tells us how to clear the many paper jams we seem to be able to create. The important point about explicit knowledge is that many of the initial iterations of knowledge management dealt solely with explicit knowledge. But this is the easiest part of any knowledge management initiative and the one most amenable to networked computer solutions. Think about the databases, customer contact lists, process manuals, organisational procedural documents, and so on that exist in your organisation. Now combine them into one large electronic exchange, searchable by staff anywhere, and you see what we mean. The knowledge management dream has been to create some kind of exchange that allows everyone in the organisation to be able to access the collected know-how, experience, and wisdom of the entire company. In Stewart's words (1999:113), this is 'the dream of creating what amount to living libraries containing an entire stock of corporate knowledge.'

Missing Knowledge

A third category of knowledge relevant to human capital is the 'missing knowledge'. This is the knowledge that your staff need to do their jobs (both today and in the future) that they currently do not have. We introduce the notion of missing knowledge here to underscore the point that any knowledge management strategy must take account of your future knowledge needs if your business is to survive. Missing knowledge might fit into our taxonomy of human capital in the following way:

Increasing awareness	You know what you don't know **Active Missing Knowledge**	You know what you know **Explicit Knowledge**
	You don't know what you don't know **Passive Missing Knowledge**	You don't know what you know **Tacit Knowledge**

Increasing knowledge

Clearly, the challenge for organisations is to create mechanisms that enable them to transform their passive missing knowledge into active missing knowledge (by becoming aware of what it is they don't know they don't know) and working to fill those knowledge gaps.

Structural Capital

To expect a man to retain everything that he has ever read is like expecting him to carry about in his body everything that he has ever eaten.
– ARTHUR SCHOPENHAUER

Structural capital describes systems used to manage the intellect of your staff and convert it into useful products and services. Leif Edvinsson describes structural capital as those mechanisms which 'embody, empower, and support' human capital (1997). Knowledge management is about the sharing and transporting of knowledge around an organisation so that the knowledge can be leveraged to provide some sort of competitive advantage. Doing this requires structural intellectual assets, and these constitute your organisation's structural capital. Indeed, the term includes anything that helps turn individual know-how into knowledge for the organisation as a whole. It commonly includes things like:

- the organisational culture;
- the organisational structure;
- the management philosophy;
- management processes;
- quality standards;

○ information resources (such as databases, a corporate library, process manuals, etc.) and
○ any patents held, design rights, trade secrets (and anything that is copyright).

One way that organisations maximise the value of their structural capital is to embed the best ideas from their staff (best practice) into the day-to-day operational procedures of the organisation. Like people, organisations brim with tacit knowledge – 'intuitions, rules of thumb, mind-sets, unwritten rules of turf and territory, unconscious values', and so on (Stewart, 1999:72). The challenge here is to assess this tacit knowledge, and then find a way to leverage it. Note here that many organisations thrive by creating smart systems rather than employing smart people. Or, to put this another way, employing smart people alone will not necessarily make for a smart organisation. You only need to think about your average university to see this: a collection of highly qualified (and often even quite bright) people but an organisation that is hardly a paragon of collective brilliance. Compare this to an organisation like McDonald's where the existence of smart organisational systems guarantees consistent standards regardless of where you buy the food (or who prepares it). Another good example of such structural capital at work is the sales system used at the GAP clothing stores. This system, called the GAP-ACT system, structures the way that GAP sales staff greet the customer, approach them, initiate the sale, up-sell, and close the sale. Derived from thousands of sales, GAP-ACT is best practice at its most severe: it is a 'complete sales system that is so finely honed that it can be taught in its entirety in a single afternoon' (Rushkoff, 1999:61). Taking the knowledge out of the heads of the best staff and putting it into the rules of the system means that 'investment in training is kept to a minimum, and the skill level required to enact the selling system is low enough for the average high school student to be able to carry it off' (*Ibid.*).

Both McDonald's Speedee system and Gap's GAP-ACT system are extreme cases of structural capital at work (because they are designed to function perfectly with minimal human capital inputs) but, in most cases, the relationship between structural and human capital is more interdependent. Human capital is what builds structural capital, but the better your structural capital, the better your human capital is likely to be.

Customer / Supplier Capital

Customer and supplier capital is often presented in terms of the likelihood that your customers (and suppliers) will keep doing business with you. The way to increase this likelihood is to build a closer relationship with your customers and suppliers, and you build those relationships through better meeting their needs. Wal-Mart, which is often used as an example of maximising customer/supplier capital, describe their suppliers as 'an extension of the company' and predict that 'all retailers will eventually work this way' (*The Economist*, 8 December 2001:60).

In finding out how to meet those needs, though, you will discover that your customers and suppliers know a great deal about your organisation and how to make it run smarter. The suggestions they will offer will have implications that stretch much deeper into your organisation than simply the interface between your organisation and theirs. To the extent that listening to what your suppliers and customers tell you will increase the likelihood that they will continue to do business with you, you can think of customer/supplier capital as a direct way of turning intellectual capital into profits. Interestingly, the nature of this relationship is the one intangible value that traditional accounting has always readily acknowledged, labelling it 'goodwill', and willingly ascribed a monetary value.

ALL EYES ON THE DOOR?

A participant in one of our courses about knowledge management explained the difference between human, structural, and customer capital in the following way. She said: 'Human capital is what walks out the door at the end of the day. Structural capital is everything they leave behind when the lights go off. And Customer capital is why they all come back to work the next day.'

This chapter has attempted to define the most common concepts used when talking about knowledge management. Some other terms and concepts that you are likely to read in this book are explained in the glossary on page 175.

chapter four

Drowning in Information?

Or, Why Knowledge Management is Not About IT

What is needed is skill rather than machinery.
– WILBUR WRIGHT

Consider The Bay Of Pigs ...

There is an interesting scene in the movie *Thirteen Days*, about how the Kennedy Administration dealt with the Cuban missile crisis, where JFK asks his joint chiefs of staff what he should do next. Their advice is that the US should start bombing Cuba. In case the bombing raids fail to dissuade the Cubans from basing the Soviet ballistic missiles on their soil, then the air raids should be followed up with an invasion of the island (and, if the Soviet Union should take umbrage at this, then a policy of 'managed' escalation that might lead all the way to World War Three). This scene is interesting because, on one level at least, it seems so absurd: seeking a solution to a policy problem, JFK asks the heads of his military about his options. The joint chiefs, of course, instead offer a military solution. Not once (in the movie at least) did the joint chiefs insist that negotiation, diplomacy, and compromise would be the wise counsel. In many regards, none of this is surprising: we have all heard the old saw that 'to the person with a hammer, every problem looks like a nail that needs hammering.' The surprise in *Thirteen Days* is not that the joint chiefs saw the solution in some mix of blockade, bombardment, and invasion, but that the President sought their advice hoping for any other kind of answer. The solutions the joint chiefs offered are an expression of what is known as 'path dependency' (see note 7, page 173). This is the idea that how we solve our current problems will be determined by the solutions we have tried in the past. Path dependency is not only something that skews presidential policy advice but is common in all walks of life. For instance, it is apparent in medicine, where surgeons are notorious for suggesting that the solution to any medical problem is some sort of surgical intervention.

The notion of path dependency is relevant to knowledge management because, we believe, it explains why the first generation of knowledge management solutions relied so heavily on information technology (IT). Believing that knowledge was a commodity like information or data, many organisations turned to their IT people and asked how best to capture and communicate their knowledge assets. The IT people, being IT people, suggested that computers were the obvious way to solve this problem. We saw in the last chapter how computers are certainly able to help with storing, codifying, and communicating explicit knowledge. But they are not as good at dealing with tacit knowledge, and next to no use when it comes to ensuring that staff actually internalise the knowledge available on the network. A study of this 'first generation' of knowledge management, conducted in 1997 by Ernst and Young and involving 432 companies, revealed that most of the efforts made by those companies involved investing in some form of knowledge repository (such as intranets and data warehouses), building networks so that people could find each other, and implementing technologies to facilitate collaboration. But, as Pfeffer and Sutton (1999) note, 'these are all activities that treat knowledge pretty much like steel or any other resource, to be gathered, shared, and distributed.' What was missing from these first generation efforts were the strategies to integrate that knowledge into what staff actually do.

Lest we be misunderstood, let us be clear that we think information technology is an essential element of a successful knowledge management strategy. The point we want to make in this chapter is that information technology *alone* will never, and can never, be sufficient for a successful knowledge management strategy. As Jack Gordon put it, 'while knowledge management operates via computer systems, it is not about computers – and it cannot be if it is to be effective. It has to be about learning' (1999:30). This remains an important point because too many organisations continue to put too much faith in technology as a panacea for knowledge management. A simple metric of this imbalance can be seen in the proportion of knowledge management budgets that is allocated to technology. Thomas Davenport and Larry Prusak (1998:78) have a 'thirty-three-and-a-third rule' to help organisations keep their projects in perspective. This rule tells us that if more than a third of the total time and money resources of a project is spent on technology, then it's an IT project and not a knowledge management one.

Focusing your knowledge management efforts on technology can prove to be futile because, clearly, what really matters is *what* is communicated (and what your staff *do* with that) and not *how* it is communicated. Marshall McLuhan was wrong – the medium is *not* the message. Davenport and Prusak use the example of the telephone, noting that having a telephone 'does not guarantee or even encourage brilliant conversations' (1998:4). At some levels, we all know this about computers – and even the IT people remind us of the GIGO principle (that if you put 'garbage in' to your computer system, then you will only ever get 'garbage out') – but there is still a tendency to be seduced by the promise of the technology. Let's have a brief look at how that promise has turned out to be false.

The Limits of Technology: Where Did All The Productivity Go?

We have transformed information into a form of garbage.
– NEIL POSTMAN

One of the most startling facts about information technology is that there is very little evidence that it has had any measurable effect on our productivity. Stop and think about that sentence for a moment – because, if you are anything like us, it will probably strike you as an absurd claim. How can computers not have made us all more productive? Even the very fact we are writing this book on our laptops and desktops, and not with pens and paper, has to put the lie to this claim, right? The data suggest not. Indeed, it is because the evidence reveals something that flies in the face of our commonsense view that this phenomenon has been labelled 'the productivity paradox'.

Nor is this the view of merely a small group of disaffected Luddites: the former head of information technology at Xerox, Paul Strassman, argued back in 1997 that 'there is no correlation between expenditures for information technologies and any known measures of profitability' (quoted in Jonscher, 2000:188). It is a position supported by a number of research projects carried out at MIT, most famously by Robert Solow, the Nobel Laureate economist, who summarised that 'we see computers everywhere except in the productivity statistics' (quoted in Jonscher, 2000:189). The data are clear: the investment made in information technology has not repaid the productivity gains promised of it. In contrast, investment in new production technologies (plant) pays unmistakable gains, and of a kind that are simply not apparent from the investment in IT.

HOW MUCH WILL COMPUTERS CHANGE OUR LIVES?

Charles Jonscher is clear: 'I have gleaned two lessons from the history, short as it has been, of electronic technology ... the first is to regard almost any prediction of the future power of the technology itself as understated. The second is to regard almost any prediction of what it will do to our everyday lives as overstated' (2000:248). Douglas Coupland, in his iconoclastic book *Generation X: Tales for an Accelerated Culture*, talks about the growth in 'cryptotechnophobia' – 'the secret belief that technology is more of a menace than a boon'.

Although the 'productivity paradox' has become increasingly recognised of late, this is not a new argument. As long ago as 1986, Theodore Roszak was pointing out the negative impacts of computers in *The Cult of Information*. Roszak argued that 'our capacity to think about [the] world is being undermined by the very "information" that is supposed to help us understand it. Data processing replaces thought; "data glut" obscures basic questions ...'

Those who defend the productivity dividend of computers respond to the paradox in two ways. The first is the classic 'We need to wait longer for the gains to become apparent,' (see note 8, page 173) and the second is that we are not looking closely enough at the figures. We can respond to the first criticism by noting that we don't actually have the time to wait, and to the second by noting that if we have to look that hard to find the gain then its magnitude is clearly out of all proportion to the investment made (see note 9, page 174).

We need to note that this argument is not about whether computers have made certain aspects of our lives easier but about whether the total effect of computers on our lives has been as productive as we might otherwise think. In other words, many of the 'efficiencies' achieved are either illusory or are negated by a decrease in efficiency somewhere else. The most obvious example of this is the way that computers tend to replace one category of worker with another. As Edward Tenner puts it:

> You can find one group [of staff] trained to accomplish things the old-fashioned way. Or you can pay another group to set up and maintain machines and systems that will do the same work with fewer employees – of the older category of worker' (1997:245).

For instance, consider the example of financial management: the advent of computerised bookkeeping means that organisations can get by with fewer accountants but, often, needing more programmers and systems support people than initially anticipated. Nor is this a trivial point: the automobile factories of Detroit now spend more on the information technology needed to support their office functions (management, marketing, accounting, etc.) than they do on the automation of the factories themselves. Similarly, hospitals in the US spend more on the computers they use for administration than they do on those in the wards and operating theatres (all Jonscher, 2000:201).

Moreover, much computer 'support' is, in practice, provided by competent users within organisations. It's the smart guy down the hall who becomes an important resource even though he has had nothing added to his job description. The hidden cost here being the time that guy takes out from his real job to help others. The more organisations attempt to introduce computer systems without adequate, formalised support systems in place, the more these informal peer support mechanisms need to expand to take their place. Research carried out by the Boston consulting company Nolan, Norton, and Co. argues that these 'hidden' costs of peer support contribute the lion's share of the total cost of computing within an organisation (in Tenner, 1997:253).

Another argument about why information technology doesn't correlate well with gains in productivity highlights the dislocation caused by the many rapid changes in that technology. By the time your staff have finally learned how to use one system, a replacement system is being introduced. We saw in chapter one how quickly the hardware changes. But add to this the updated versions of the various software products, the raft of organisational changes that redefine what the system is supposed to provide, and the changing market demands, and it is a wonder much gets done at all. To take one example, the IT systems guru we introduced in chapter one (with the GPS-equipped car), has gone from an Apple Newton to a Palm Pilot to an IPac in the three years we have been working with him. Although we acknowledge that he is a special case (if it's hi-tech and new, the chances are he'll be at the head of the queue), all of us have had to deal with the change from CD-ROMs to online databases, and from e-mails to web presences to e-commerce. Think of it like this: If these developments were supposed to save time, then where did all that saved time go?

PRESS ONE FOR MORE OPTIONS ...

Pico Iyer writes about a friend of his who is tied into a dazzling array of communication networks: e-mail, voice-mail, mobile phone, land-line phone, fax, pager, and so on, but Iyer

> couldn't help but notice that most of the messages he received seemed to have to do with the difficulty of receiving messages. The state-of-the-art communications facilities seemed to be [most] adept at communicating communications mishaps. 'Resend' reverberated around the office, and 'abort'. 'Your call is being diverted' said his phone; 'Your call is being transferred.' (2000:100)

But perhaps the best argument to explain the 'productivity paradox' is the simplest: computers, despite all their high tech wizardry, simply do not make us any more productive. In the words of Ricardo Semler: 'Everything has become excessively complicated and confused, which is exactly the condition [that] computers were supposed to remedy.' One part of this argument stresses the limited applicability of computers in real world situations, pointing out that computers are good at dealing with highly specific tasks but are easily fooled by ambiguity. This is no surprise when we realise that 'the quality we call common sense, the ability to respond to a situation in a completely unstructured manner, actually requires much greater levels of mental agility and prior experience than the specific tasks in expert systems' (Jonscher, 2000:142). For a fascinating insight into what this means for the day-to-day life of your organisation, check out Ian Parker's article on PowerPoint in the May 2001 issue of *The New Yorker*. Parker's article, which should be mandatory reading for anyone interested in knowledge management, poses the question 'Can a software package edit our thoughts?' His answer is unequivocal.

An obvious way that computers make us less productive is that they are so good at what they do well. Because the technology makes it so easy to access and share information, the amount of information the average information worker receives in a day is staggering (and, often, distracting). Think about the number of e-mails your staff receive each day, consider what that does for the rhythm of their working day, and imagine how many of the e-mails they receive and send are not related to work. Or try this: how many e-mails do you delete without reading from your own in-box? Add to this mix the messages left for you with your secretary, on your mobile phone, through the fax, via paper memos and letters, and even through Post-It notes stuck to your office door. The proliferation of information everywhere means we are simultaneously experiencing both a data flood *and* a data drought. Because there is so much information (the flood), we are increasingly incapable of finding the key piece of information we are looking for (the drought). This not only has an adverse effect on our productivity but, for many of us, it is also having a material effect on our professional and private lives.

DYING FOR INFORMATION?

In October 1996, Reuters carried out a study into information overload, involving 1300 managers in the UK, USA, Hong Kong and Singapore. The report of this study, *Dying for Information?*, revealed the extent to which 'information overload' has become a problem for professionals. The findings include:

- *Time is wasted:* 38% of managers surveyed said they wasted 'substantial' amounts of time just looking for information; 47% of respondents said that information collection distracts them from their main responsibilities.
- *Decisions are often delayed:* 43% of respondents thought that decisions were delayed and otherwise adversely affected by 'analysis paralysis' or the existence of too much information.
- *Working life suffers:* Two out of three respondents associated information overload with tension with colleagues and loss of job satisfaction.
- *Personal life suffers:* 42% of respondents attributed ill-health to this stress; 61% said that they have to cancel social activities as a result of information overload and 60% that they are frequently too tired for leisure activities (all Reuters, 1997).
- Most surprisingly (and worst of all), it was mainly for nothing: most believed they were 'submerged under piles of information but starved of knowledge'. The study concluded that people can no longer develop effective personal strategies for managing information. Faced with an onslaught of information and information channels, they have become unable to develop simple routines for managing information.

There is an important lesson here for knowledge management: Whatever system an organisation adopts, it has to do more than simply accumulate information. If not, the amount of information in the system will quickly outstrip the ability of users to engage with it. Our favourite example here is the National Security Agency in the United

States. This intelligence gathering agency 'has the technical ability to intercept and store enough information to wallpaper much of the planet [but] what is in doubt is the agency's ability to make sense of most of it' (Doder, 2001:25). After all, this is the same agency which mistakenly verified the North Vietnamese involvement in the Gulf of Tonkin incident (thus precipitating the United States' involvement in Vietnam), failed to predict the collapse of the Soviet Union, was incapable of locating Suddam Hussein's Scud missiles, and was taken by surprise by India's nuclear tests in 1998. All this despite the fact that the NSA classifies between 50 and 100 million documents every year – more than all other agencies of the US government combined.

The lesson for all organisations here is that any knowledge management system needs to actively synthesise, summarise, assess, *and purge* the content of the system. This 'data reduction' role cannot be overemphasised. A number of commentators have stressed that this is where technology can now offer the most assistance – to help limit the amount of information that users get exposed to. For instance, Eli Noam from Columbia University noted: 'The real issue for future technology does not appear to be production of information, and certainly not transmission. Almost anybody can add information. The difficult question is how to reduce it' (quoted in Shenk, 1997:29).

It is here that the discipline of knowledge management has much to add to any system that attempts to effectively share knowledge.

Field of Dreams?

What was the means has become the ends ... instead of helping us organize data, computers are drowning us in it.
– RICARDO SEMLER

Not only does the technology have inherent limits, but clearly no information technology system can increase productivity where staff do not engage with it. This is an important point for knowledge management because many IT designers follow the *Field of Dreams* approach – that 'if you build it, they will come.' In contrast, there is a considerable body of research that deals with how technology is defined, used, and evaluated by those that are tasked with adopting it. Not surprisingly, the evidence is clear that this *Field of Dreams* approach rarely succeeds as expected.

According to the conventional model, experts define the parameters of the system and make a series of assumptions about how users will adopt and apply that system. Users are then taught how to use the system, and the adoption and integration of the system into pre-existing patterns of work is assumed to be unproblematic. Once in place, the new system drives broader changes in workplace behaviour and attitudes consistent with the values embedded in the system. An easy way to picture this approach is that the experts who define and design the system simply throw the completed system over the wall to users. These users then, after a period of training and experimentation, engage with the system and integrate it into their working lives. This perspective is known as technological determinism, because it sees technology as the key driver of organisational form and change.

WHAT DO YOU MEAN 'YOU CAN'T WRITE CODE'?

Todd Campbell of ABCNEWS.com argues that one of the biggest problems with computers is that they are much harder to use than they should be. Although acknowledging that things have improved somewhat in recent years, he still maintains that – for the average user – many basic tasks are 'either counterintuitive or just plain mysterious.' Campbell argues that one of the reasons for this is that the engineers and programmers who design the systems do not value simplicity. This is because (i) their peers are impressed by attributes other than usability, and (ii) they are so steeped in the technology that 'they find it impossible to believe that novice users weren't born knowing, for example, how to attach a file to an e-mail message.' Campbell adds 'when testing reveals that a given task is difficult for the average user to execute, software developers generally just shake their heads and wonder why people are so stupid instead of wondering why computers are so complicated' (all from 'The Answer Geek' at www.abcnews.com).

In contrast to this conventional (determinist) view, the emerging best practice model places much more emphasis on the contribution that users can make in the areas of defining, designing, and disseminating the new technological system. In this view, the emphasis is very much on the 'social life' of the technology required by end users and on being clear about how the new system will merge with that social life. In this regard, users are seen much more as co-producers of the system rather than merely as consumers of it. This perspective is known as social constructionism because it emphasises the role that the organisational context plays in shaping how technology is actually used.

In retrospect, social constructionism can be seen to make a great deal of sense. For instance, the conventional (technologically deterministic) view can be seen to impose systems on users from the top down, whereas the social life approach enables systems to grow from the bottom up; in the conventional view, resistance to the new system requires the identification of barriers among users (which are then conceptualised as mere teething troubles, soluble through recourse to minor systems modifications or better training) whereas the 'constructivist' view builds its dissemination strategy from the identification of the needs of its users; finally, the conventional approach often leads to systems being used by staff for very different purposes from those the designers intended, whereas the social life view ensures the designers and users are clear about both what is required and what is practicable. What is important about the constructivist view is that it highlights the key role that workplace culture plays in the long-term success (that is, adoption, integration, and use) of any new technological system.

TECHNOLOGICAL DETERMINISM

The idea that technology determines, or shapes, the social organisation that grows around it. This view sees technology as an objective, external force that users have to adapt to. 'If you build it, they will come', and you can shape the behaviour you want from the kind of system you build. The technology is paramount.

SOCIAL CONSTRUCTIONISM

Focuses on 'the human action' aspect of technology and on how the shared interpretations of the meaning of a certain technology arise and affect the development of, and interaction with, that technology. The organisational culture (the 'social life' of the technology) is paramount.

It follows from the foregoing discussion that the key to successful integration of technology is workplace culture. There is a critical need to include users in the definition, design, and dissemination of the system. But once the system has been 'rolled out', there are ongoing key roles that users can play in supporting (and spreading) the system among each other. For instance, there is now considerable research evidence that making any technological system *actually* work involves skills that do not appear in textbooks or procedural manuals (for instance, see Tenner, 1997:252). In other words, that the adoption and integration of technology involves coming to terms with an embedded culture and its existing skill sets. This means there will be a collection of key system champions within the organisation who can make a significant contribution to ensuring the eventual success of the system. Equally, there will be key opinion leaders (of which the champions are likely to be an important subset) that will also contribute to the system's success through their word-of-mouth endorsement or censure. Indeed, it is precisely because the technology needs to succeed in this kind of environment that it is so important to ensure these opinion leaders are engaged from the outset, and equally, that such opinion leaders (and key staff – such as the CEO) are seen to use the system. This may sound like simply common sense but, as Christine Rollo and Thomas Clarke remind us, in practice: 'Companies tend to invest in technology rather than attempting the organisational and cultural change needed to promote knowledge transition and circulation' (2001:11).

What Can Computers Offer Knowledge Management?

Any intelligent fool can make things bigger [and] more complex, [but] it takes a touch of genius – and a lot of courage – to move in the opposite direction.
– E F SCHUMACHER

The argument of this book is that any knowledge management strategy needs to be concerned with the *quality* of information flowing around the organisation and not the quantity; and with the *timeliness* of information delivery, not its speed. By contrast, information technologies have historically been sold on the basis of their storage capacity (their ability to store vast quantities of information) and their processor rate (the speed with which they can operate). Equally, knowledge management – ultimately – is about learning (we identify knowledge, store it, and communicate it, so that staff can apply it to their work). In Charles Jonscher's words, 'deep down, the information revolution is not about technology working with data but about people working with knowledge' (2000:26). Consequently, computers are useful in knowledge management to the extent that they effectively support learning. As the OECD has noted, 'knowledge and information tend to be abundant; what is scarce is the capacity to use them in meaningful ways' (1996:11).

The key, then, is to introduce a knowledge management system in tandem with broader changes to organisational culture (see chapter five). What matters is not how much is spent but how well those efforts are focused. There are two broad approaches that can be taken here – one of codification (which concentrates on ways to codify and store knowledge in computer databases), and one of personalisation (where the emphasis is on connecting people with other people so they can communicate and share the knowledge they need).

Codifying Knowledge: The Way of the Database

Too often travel, instead of broadening the mind, merely lengthens the conversation.
- ELIZABETH DEW

As we have already seen, one of the obvious ways that information technologies can support knowledge management is through the creation of a database to store the explicit knowledge that exists within an organisation. These kinds of databases are known as universal databases because they manage data in many different forms (letters, documents, spreadsheets, images, video clips, etc.) Done well, such databases can pay big returns. In one US study, it was found that 'the average organization earned a three-year return on its investment of 179 per cent, much of it attributed to reduced cost and time of internal communications and improved tracking and administration of projects' (Stewart, 1999:113). As well as providing a mechanism that enables staff to tap into their colleagues' knowledge, databases provide a useful way for coping with growth and staff turnover. Some kind of living database, in tandem with a staff mentoring programme, is an important component of effective organisational memory.

THE DATABASE AT PHILIPS FOX

In 1998, Philips Fox won a silver medal at the Giga Excellence Awards for Innovation for 'FoxTrek', its in-house knowledge management database. This system, developed in Philips Fox's Sydney office, was designed to provide its staff with 'a platform-independent, single point of access to the knowledge held across the firm.' The ultimate aim was 'to reduce the time spent on research and to capture the knowledge and experience of [the] senior lawyers for the benefit of new, or younger, lawyers and all clients ... That is, to preserve our valuable legal memory.' FoxTrek works by accessing information from existing repositories (such as the firm's document management system, library database, selected websites used for research, and the company's intranet) and bringing this to the firm's lawyers via a browser and accessed through a tailored research page on the corporate intranet. According to Philips Fox's Technology Director, 'the absolute key criteria (sic) for development of FoxTrek was being able to provide the information through one interface to all staff. Using one search question, they are able to find what they want.' Having the system in place 'avoids the duplication of research efforts and allows lawyers to share their expertise and knowledge with other lawyers in their practice group or enterprise wide' (all www.phillipsfox.com.au).

Our own suggestions about what to put into a knowledge management database (see chapter six) are deliberately modest. By contrast, too many organisations are overly ambitious: they believe that everything within the organisation should be put online. This is clearly a mistake because, by overwhelming staff with more knowledge than they could ever use, they effectively reduce knowledge to data. There is a tension for the CKO (or knowledge manager) here: they are eager to prove the worth of their knowledge management system and may wish to do this by expanding it rather than restricting it. But — trust us — in this instance *less is more*. Knowledge managers must work to ensure the stocks of knowledge available to the organisation contain relevant knowledge and that the means for keeping that knowledge flowing do not overwhelm staff with trivia.

DOES 'SMART TECHNOLOGY' MAKE US DUMBER?

Does having access to all that 'smart' technology have a negative effect on our ability to reason and remember? If you had asked us 15 years ago, we would have laughed at the thought, dismissing the idea as readily as we dismissed those elementary school teachers who told us that using calculators — instead of learning our multiplication tables by rote — would stunt our intelligence. Five years ago we might have reluctantly acknowledged that spell-checkers and grammar-checkers did seem to have a negative impact on the language skills of the students we taught (or, as we read in a recent *National Business Review*, that 'it was ironic that while telecommunications formed an integral part of modern technology, the art of communication was being lost' [Raman, 2001:46]). Last year, we might have argued that it could all be explained by generational effects (whatever technology we use merely assists and reinforces our natural intelligence, whatever technology subsequent generations use atrophies their brains). But, this year, we came across a study that suggests the techno-sceptics were right all along. This study, carried out by Hokkaido University in Japan, provides a convincing argument that the reliance on automatic memory (in computers, PDAs, mobile phones, etc.) has a negative impact on neural development. The study found that 10 per cent of those studied who were 25 to 35 years old had severe memory problems, and that this lifestyle-related dysfunction was completely separate from the normal deterioration brought about by ageing (*CPUniverse.com's Weekly Review*, 5 February 2001). Pass me my Ipac so I can remember to make a note about this!

Personalisation: Using the Technology to Make Connections

Companies will no longer be proud of how extensive their knowledge portals are, but rather of how targeted an information environment they create.
– THOMAS DAVENPORT AND JOHN BECK

The important reservation that accompanies databasing knowledge is that the system will only work if staff consult the database. The evidence from research, and from our own experience, suggests that staff are likely to use their own networks before they turn to formal records like databases. When faced with a difficult question, staff are 'much much more likely to go to people they respect and avail themselves of their knowledge than they are to look for information in databases ... most people in organizations consult a few knowledgeable people when they need expert advice on a particular subject' (Davenport and Prusak, 1998:12). Ask yourself: What do you do when you want to know something in your own organisation? Where do you turn when you find yourself needing to know something novel?

Given this propensity to tap into existing social networks of knowledge, there is a strong argument for creating knowledge management systems that connect people with one another. This is the approach that argues the technology is only 'the pipeline and storage system for the knowledge exchange' (Davenport and Prusak, 1998:18). The key is to find ways to get the technology to support knowledge creating and knowledge sharing systems, not the other way around. One powerful way to do this is through the creation of an online 'knowledge map' that identifies where the expertise resides in your organisation. This knowledge map, often called the 'Yellow Pages', for obvious reasons, is then made accessible to everyone in the organisation. Also, the technology allows the 'Yellow Pages' to hyperlink to more detailed entries, or even to an online video of the person in question. Lotus Notes and some kind of web browser-intranet have been common tools used for corporate knowledge maps.

DOCUSHARE FROM XEROX

One approach to building the 'Yellow Pages' kind of knowledge map is with DocuShare from Xerox. This is a combined document, video, audio, and graphics management system running on a web-based platform, owned and maintained by users. Designed with communities of practice in mind, DocuShare provides an easy-to-use approach to managing pertinent information. As *InfoWorld* noted:

> Groupware solutions do not offer DocuShare's document capabilities. Lotus, for example, recognizing the complexity of its Notes software, has introduced its QuickPlace teamware solution, and Instinctive Software's eRoom provides document sharing and interactive functions, including polls. But these solutions target interactive teamwork, offering document sharing only to support online collaboration. DocuShare, however, is designed specifically to handle large data libraries (Heck, 1999).

Searching for the 'Killer App' ...

It isn't that they can't see the solution. It is that they can't see the problem.
– G K CHESTERTON

The implicit message of this chapter is not to believe that any information technology product can solve all your knowledge management needs (and, moreover, not to believe anyone who says they can). In short, there are no 'killer apps' for knowledge management but, as we have seen, there are lots of ways to kill the application of knowledge. In place of the panacea of a killer app, there are a number of 'best practice' lessons that any system design needs to take into consideration.

Best Practice Lessons

1. Enrol Users in the Design of the System

We have talked at length about the value of enrolling end users in the definition, design, and dissemination of the system in order to ensure their 'ownership' and use of it. There is nothing to add here except to say 'Do so'.

2. Aim for Just-in-Time Delivery

Combating information overload is a surprisingly difficult undertaking. One approach that we have seen organisations adopt is to mechanically purge content from the system. For instance, automatically deleting any e-mails that remain in a staff member's in-box for more than 30 days (and deleting any e-mail in any folder that is over 12 months old). The problem with such approaches is that they cannot discriminate between meaningful content and spam, and that they work at the wrong end of the information–user chain (that is, after staff have downloaded information from the system). An alternative is to use some kind of 'intelligent' 'bot' to filter the information before the end user is exposed to it (a simple example is the filters available in most e-mail programmes that stop your Uncle Ira from sending through his joke of the day). But these, too, are remarkably blunt instruments. (What happens if – just once – your Uncle Ira sends through some startling insight that would have proved of tremendous value if only the filter hadn't deleted it sight unseen?)

A much more desirable approach is to create systems that distinguish between information that is **pushed** on to someone and the information that they **pull** from the organisation's stocks. Effective knowledge management needs to make it easy for staff to pull the knowledge they need from the system, at the same time as restrict the amount of information that is pushed on to them. The difference between pushed and pulled information is the same as that between just-in-case (JIC) and just-in-time (JIT) inventory control. Indeed, successful knowledge management can be seen as moving the organisation from storing information just in case it is needed by someone, somewhere, to an organisation that enables staff to access the knowledge they need just in time to solve the problems they confront.

THE CURSE OF FYI

The classic case of information that is pushed on to staff is the FYI circulation. Once upon a time, this involved mostly photocopies of articles, memos, or briefing papers that other staff members thought you might find of interest (hence the 'for your interest' tag). One of the authors, Carl, used to work in a large research organisation whose CEO had a habit of circulating anything she had read that her staff might find interesting. When Carl left that organisation, he took with him a box piled high with the FYI articles, which remained stubbornly unread. (As Carl says: 'I always meant to read them, and lots of them did look interesting and relevant to my job, it's just that there were so many other demands on my time.') In the decade since then, the opportunities to share things FYI have increased rapidly (think of forwarding e-mails, passing on URLs, or the 'share this article with a friend' facility that many web pages offer). The technology provides endless ways to push information at others. We should be honest here and note that even we find it surprisingly difficult to resist this temptation.

3. Focus on the Quality of Information, not its Quantity

One way to resist the temptation to push information on to users is to limit the amount of information in the system. And the best way to do this is to leave only the highest quality information available to staff. If this is not practical, then at least ensure that you feed a few pieces of information to your staff at a time. People are much better at dealing with information fed to them in small parcels over time than they are when it comes in a large collection all at once (Davenport and Beck, 2001:67). James Fallows provides an important warning of what can happen where neither of these approaches is taken. Talking about changes to the profession of journalism, he writes 'the danger of the data-central approach is precisely that it is too fast and too easy … you can collect [the data] without having any firsthand sense of what you are writing about … you are limited by the things other people have noticed and written about and are cut off from a reporter's main asset: his (sic) confidence in what he has directly observed' (Fallows, 1997:149).

4. Make Content Attractive

One way to help information and knowledge get the attention of your staff is by being especially careful how that information is presented. How to make information attractive is a well-developed field (this is what the advertising and publishing industries do all the time) but it is one that has – to date – translated poorly into the area of knowledge management. Thomas Davenport and John Beck talk about this need in their fascinating book *The Attention Economy: Understanding the New Currency of Business*. They also explicitly make the connection to knowledge management, noting:

> In the past few months, we've begun to notice several examples of knowledge management that is highly conscious of its audience's attention … [involving knowledge management philosophies] attempting either to produce more attention-getting knowledge or to protect employee attention by eliminating unnecessary distributions of knowledge and information (2001:207).

HOW TO KEEP PEOPLE USING YOUR INTRANET

Sherrill Tapsell (2001) provides five suggestions to make sure your staff keep using the intranet:
- Publish a monthly newsletter: 'These are ideal ways to keep users in touch with what's coming up and what's changing.'
- Add a quick poll: 'These polls will attract users and enable them to provide input on issues.'
- Ask them to bookmark your site: 'The simplest technique of getting repeat users.'
- Produce regular content: 'Make sure you update your content on a regular basis ... let your users know [the schedule for updating the content] so they know when to come back.'
- Add a discussion board: Create 'a common area where your users can share ideas, exchange tips, and post questions and find other people with similar interests.'

5. Aim to Connect Users with Users

Because knowledge management is ultimately about learning, a major role that technology can play is through the provision of networks that allow staff to communicate with one another. Knowledge management is not about pursuing artificial intelligence but – where possible – about getting in touch with the real thing. Creating a conduit for communication is more important than storing content.

6. Be Flexible

All knowledge management systems need to allow for the fact that knowledge is plastic: it can be modified as it is adopted and used by others. Those attempts that only frame the task of knowledge management as a process of knowledge transfer will likely fail precisely because they do not recognise that 'much of the task of managing knowledge in an organization is not only the creation and movement of knowledge to the right place, but the institution of process through which knowledge can be altered, negotiated, transformed as it moves among groups' (Carlile, 1998:58). It is important that any system not only meet the needs of users at the outset but also change as the needs of its users change. This ability of the system to grow and adapt is particularly critical in fast-moving, cutting-edge knowledge companies.

7. Keep Your Eye on the Prize

Focus your knowledge management efforts on technology that aims to

- codify bodies of knowledge that can then be transferred to others (or to preserve what might otherwise be lost); and
- connect people to data, experts, and expertise on a just-in-time basis.

Remember that technology can play a strong role in the sharing of explicit knowledge, and can help support the sharing of tacit knowledge to the extent that it facilitates and supports connections between staff.

Putting the People Back In

Automation may be great but nothing speeds up work like a waste basket.
- FRANK HODUR

We end this chapter by speculating about where the arguments developed here leave us in regard to information technology. David Shenk, whose book *Data Smog* highlights many of the dangers of misapplied technology, tells us:

> It is often said that we are on the cusp of a whole new age when intelligent machines will take over much of the work we do. I suspect that just the opposite may be true – that we are about to comprehend the true limitations of machines. Once we realize that information technology truly cannot replace human experience, that as it increases the available information it also helps devalue the meaning of each piece of information, we will be on the road to reasserting our dominance over technology (1997:199).

Charles Jonscher makes much the same point when he writes that the 'productivity paradox' contains a profound, and important, lesson:

> It is a confirmation, by way of a world-wide, trillion-dollar, trial, that it is and will be much more difficult to automate what we do with our minds than it was to automate what we do with our hands. We should see this not as a failure of technology but as a tribute to human skills.

We couldn't have said it better ourselves.

chapter five

Successful Knowledge Management

Success is relative: It is what we can make of the mess we have made of things.
– T S ELIOT

The Three Critical Components: Knowledge, Technology, Culture

In chapter four, we argued that successful knowledge management is about more than impressive computer systems. In this chapter, we make good on that argument by identifying what we see as the three critical components of a successful knowledge management strategy. These are:

- the right knowledge streams and sources feeding into the organisation
- the right technology to store and communicate that knowledge
- the right workplace culture so that staff are motivated to make use of that knowledge

These components are best represented by the following table:

Component	Purpose	Focus
Information and Knowledge	Inputs into knowledge management. Sources and streams of knowledge.	What do we need to know?
Technology	Mechanisms for the storage and communication of knowledge.	How do we keep on top of what we know?
Culture	Structures that motivate staff to share their knowledge, and to integrate the collected knowledge into their work.	How do we motivate staff to share what they know, and use what we all know?

The problem with this table is that it suggests that these three components are discrete entities. Instead, a more useful representation might be:

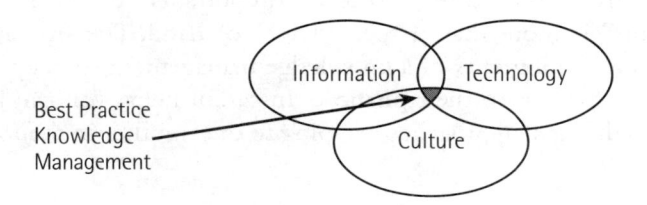

```
        Information   Technology
Best Practice
Knowledge  ─────────→
Management        Culture
```

This diagram makes it clear that successful knowledge management can only occur at the *intersection* of these three components. This is an important point because many organisations concentrate their efforts in one of these areas (for example, we saw in chapter four how some organisations attempt to pursue knowledge management through technology alone). Note too, that the use of the word 'intersection' is deliberate: what is required is that the three critical components actively come together, rather than merely overlap, in order to provide successful knowledge management.

One way to understand these three components is through the twinned notions of knowledge stocks and knowledge flows.

Knowledge Stocks and Flows

'It's a poor sort of memory that only works backwards,' the Queen remarked.
- LEWIS CARROLL, THROUGH THE LOOKING GLASS

The stocks and flows approach to knowledge management characterises the two essential dimensions of successful knowledge management as comprising:

- knowledge **stocks** – these are the things that are known. They might reside in a central repository such as a database or corporate library; scattered throughout the organisation in various offices, filing cabinets, bookshelves, and so on; or in the heads of your staff – and
- knowledge **flows**. In order to make knowledge useful (that is, in order to ensure that the knowledge that exists anywhere in the organisation is made available *everywhere* it is needed), it is

important to ensure whatever knowledge exists in the organisations is able to flow around it.

Moving from the 'three critical components' to 'two essential dimensions' is more than a mere sleight of hand. The first approach focuses on the **elements** of a knowledge management strategy whereas the second focuses on their **purpose**. In case it helps, you can think of these two different approaches mapping to one another in the following way:

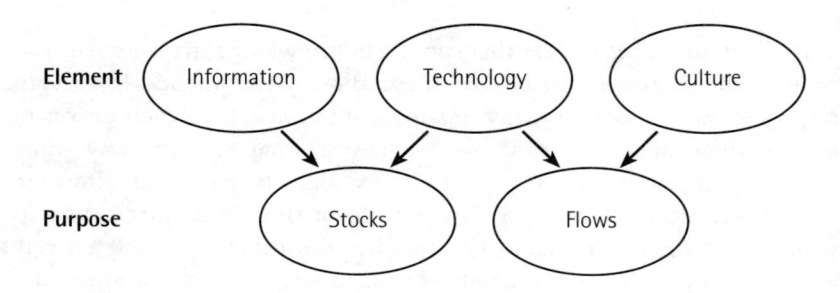

```
Element    (Information)    (Technology)    (Culture)
                  ↓   ↓            ↓   ↓
Purpose        (Stocks)          (Flows)
```

Combining these approaches in this way is useful because it provides a ready reference for (albeit, rudimentary) knowledge management troubleshooting. For instance, if you find the knowledge in your organisation simply refusing to flow to where it is needed, this model directs your attention to either the computer system in place or the culture of the organisation. Where do your own knowledge management problems reside? Do you need to increase your knowledge stocks, or is the real problem getting the knowledge you already have flowing? The stocks and flows approach also dovetails nicely with Trevor Williamson's definition of knowledge management as 'Knowledge is the stuff; management is how you get it moving.'

Increasing Knowledge Stocks

How can you increase the knowledge stocks in your organisation? Davenport and Prusak (1998) highlight six common ways that knowledge can be generated in any organisation:

- ○ **Acquisition:** as we noted in chapter three, the knowledge being managed in any organisation does not have to be new to be useful, simply new to the organisation using it. Originality is far less important than usefulness. The most obvious way that organisations acquire knowledge is by buying it. In extreme cases, this might involve buying other companies to get access to their intellectual capital (for instance IBM buying Lotus). Where knowledge is not proprietary, the easiest way to get new knowledge into the organisation is simply to copy the good ideas you have seen, heard, or read about. Some organisations have recognised the value of this 'borrowed' knowledge by giving out prizes for the best ideas brought in this way. (In chapter three we mentioned Texas Instruments, which created a 'Not Invented Here, But I Did it Anyway' award to recognise this kind of acquisition.)

- **Renting:** outside knowledge does not have to be bought outright but can be rented or leased. For instance, every time you hire a consultant you are essentially renting their knowledge. Other methods of renting might include sponsoring a research project at the local university or polytech. In every case, you need to be clear about what knowledge stays in and what knowledge leaves the organisation at the end of the contract.
- **Dedicated resources:** organisations generate knowledge by dedicating resources specifically to this purpose. R&D (research and development) departments, training units, and corporate libraries are obvious examples. The problem is that all these examples are distinct from the everyday work of an organisation. This makes transferring knowledge to the staff (where it is needed) often problematic, especially since the knowledge creators and the knowledge users (for instance, research scientists and sales managers) may not even use the same language. We outline some mechanisms for dealing with these kinds of problems in our discussion of knowledge flows, below.
- **Fusion:** knowledge often gets created at the margins of expertise, which is why it is often productive to bring staff from different divisions together to work on the same problem. The idea is that the different skills, ideas, and values will combine to create innovative solutions (and overcome the path dependency problems that can occur when you bring together a group of people who share the same assumptions).
- **Adaptation:** in the same way that some students need the pressure of a looming deadline to perform, some organisations need some sort of external threat to realise their potential. New products from competitors, new technologies, and social and economic changes all drive knowledge generation, simply

because firms that do not adapt in response to changing conditions will fail. Note, too, that success is the enemy of innovation – it is 'the winner's curse' – because it is hard to change something that has worked so well in the past. It is difficult to change a company that is struggling but it is all but impossible to change one that is showing all the outwards signs of success. Consequently, a little crisis can go a long way in the innovation stakes.
- **Networks:** knowledge is not only generated at the margins of disciplines (see above), but it is also generated at the margins of formal organisational structures. This means that the informal, self-organising networks within organisations can often be knowledge creation powerhouses. It also means that these networks of users play an important role in the total knowledge stocks available to any organisation, and should not be overlooked simply because they do not fit easily with the formal structures.

The role that workplace culture plays in supporting these six mechanisms should be clear. Firstly, each of these methods relies on recognition by managers that knowledge generation is valuable to the organisation and needs to be nurtured. Secondly, beyond simple recognition, these methods all require that staff have adequate time and space in their working lives to devote to knowledge-creating activities.

Investing in Your Staff

One significant way that organisations can increase their knowledge stocks is by educating their staff (an approach that can be seen to combine – at various times – each of the six methods listed above). This makes sense when we reflect that there are only two ways to increase the human capital available in an organisation (Stewart, 1999:86-91):

- **when the organisation uses more of what people already know:** which means creating a workplace where staff feel safe to share ideas about work, and about those they work with, without censure. In the best workplaces, the staff consider it an imperative to share their ideas.
- **when more people know more things useful to the organisation:** the easiest way to do this is to employ more experienced and/or smarter people. But this is not always practicable (if the labour market is tight), and nor will it be enough on its own (because those new people will want to feel

that knowledge sharing is reciprocal). Which means that organisations that take knowledge sharing seriously will need to invest in the continuing education of their staff. As Steve Jobs said about his time at Apple: 'it doesn't make sense to hire smart people and then tell them what to do; we hired smart people so they could tell us what to do' (in Davenport and Prusak, 1998:50).

INVESTING IN HUMAN CAPITAL

Educating staff often gets a bad reputation because employers worry that they will end up subsidising the development of their competitors' workforce. Our own experience with MBA teaching, for instance, suggests employers suspect their investment in their staff may never be repaid. There are undoubtedly examples which underscore this concern, but there is a bigger point here – that there is no doubt educating staff leads to productivity gains. Thomas Stewart cites a study carried out by the National Center on the Education Quality of the Workforce (EQW), involving more than 3000 American workplaces. This research demonstrated that educating staff was the single most effective way to increase productivity. On average, a 10 per cent increase in education led to an 8.6 per cent gain in productivity. In contrast, a 10 per cent rise in capital stock increased productivity by just 3.4 per cent (Stewart, 1999:85). In other words, the marginal value of investing in human capital is about three times greater than the value of investing in machinery.

The value of educating staff is beyond question, but it only works where that education is tailored to meet the staff's needs. Instead of rigid training regimes, what are needed are opportunities for staff to learn skills that they can actually use. Most mass audience training programmes suffer from the fact that they are pitched either too high or too low for the participants. We have all heard stories about how university professors are encouraged to repeat all the significant points of their lectures three times: once for the diligent students in the front row; once more for the average students in the middle rows; and then one last time for the hard-of-learning students in the back. Even when the message is repeated in three distinctly different ways, each repetition estranges a different part of the audience. By contrast, targeted training can be delivered once **competency maps** have been compiled for the staff. These 'maps' are records of the skills the staff need to do their jobs or further their careers (involving a current skills audit, a position skills audit, and an analysis of the gaps between the two). Once complete, the maps can be used to devolve the responsibility for 'filling in the gaps' to the staff (drawing on either in-house training resources or budgets).

MAPPING COMPETENCIES

Competency maps, as the name suggests, show the knowledge capabilities and skill levels held by various members of staff. The maps also identify the required knowledge, skills, and personal traits an employee must possess in order to be successful in a given position. Recognising the gap between the two (that is, the required and the existing skill sets) provides an excellent tool for planning training programmes. The maps also provide a mechanism for linking individual skills profiles with organisational goals to ensure that the right learning gets to the right people. The skills inventory and the competency maps allow organisations to deliver the right training and learning content to ensure the best fit between staff skills sets and organisational needs. Finally, the skills inventory can also serve as input into other enterprise-wide decision making such as managing change, handling redundancies and targeting acquisitions.

Beyond education, there is an entire literature on how the structure of work can be reorganised to encourage staff to be more innovative every day (and, hence, provide a mechanism by which organisations can 'use more of what people know'). Because every organisational structure sends a message that some issues are more important than others (that is, focuses attention and energy on particular goals), structure provides 'a potent tool for directing the attention of employees and external stakeholders' (Davenport and Beck, 2001:172). To choose one obvious example, the use of **'staff improvement systems'** (SIS) as an integral part of total quality management (TQM) programmes signals to staff that their knowledge is valuable to the organisation. We were involved in researching a number of TQM programmes in the mid-1990s and noticed two distinct productivity gains provided by SIS:

- continuous incremental improvements: in one programme, over a thousand problem areas were identified and improved in a single year. The large number reflects how modest most of these improvements were but also reflects how seriously staff took the philosophy of 'kaizen' (continuous incremental improvement).
- 'big bang' projects: in another programme a group of technicians, left to their own devices, developed an in-house filtration system that saved their company half a million dollars a year in running

expenses compared to the previous system (both Perry, Davidson, and Hill, 1995).

The Ineluctable Link Between 'Informal' and 'Informed'

'Informal organisation' is defined as how things actually get done in any organisation. The informal, improvisational practices that keep organisations functioning. This is perhaps seen most clearly in the difference between what the formal job description says a staff member *should* be doing and what they *actually* do all day.

The significant point about the informal organisation is that it recognises that the way any organisation functions is different from what the organisational charts and formal job descriptions suggest. Stephen Denning describes the difference even better:

> In textbooks, the organization is often made to seem like a piece of well-greased machinery. Everybody who works in the organization knows what it is all about and is concerned principally with implementing its mission ... [in the real world] everything seems to be falling rapidly apart. A situation not far from chaos reigns. Nobody really knows what is going on (2001:41-2).

This difference between the two faces of an organisation is one of the oldest in the sociological literature (see Brown and Duguid, 2000:113). It is also a key one for successful knowledge management. It has implications for identifying where knowledge really resides, and how that knowledge is put in motion (flows) through the organisation. We will have more to say on this in chapter six. But the important point here is about the relationship between the informal face of the organisation and learning. A study carried out by the Center for Workforce Development in the United States, involving 1000 employees, reported that up to 70 per cent of all workplace learning is informal. This is the learning that is 'unbudgeted, unplanned, and uncaptured by the organization ... [it] ... occurs in dozens of daily activities, including participating in meetings, interactions with customers, supervising or being supervised, mentoring others, communicating with peers, and training others on the job' (Pfeffer and Sutton, 1999). Among the most important sources of this learning are the 'communities of practice' that occur throughout any organisation. These communities are defined as tightknit groups formed by people working together on the same or similar tasks, and described them as a key component of knowledge management because of the role they play in creating and transferring knowledge.

Thomas Stewart takes it a stage further and calls communities of practice 'the shop floor of human capital, the place where the stuff gets made.' This is because real-world learning occurs within groups of people with like-minded goals (that is, learning is a social activity). And because communities of practice emerge spontaneously, they are beyond normal managerial control. He states:

> Communities of practice are responsible only to themselves. No-one owns them ... they emerge of their own accord [where staff] collaborate directly, use one another for sounding boards, teach each other, strike out together to explore new subject matter ... you cannot create communities like this by fiat, but they are easy to destroy. They are among the most important structures of any organization where thinking matters; but they are, almost inevitably, subversive of its formal structures and strictures (Stewart, 1999:96).

Given that communities of practice play such a significant role in creating and transferring knowledge, the important question must be 'How can an organisation develop them?' This is a trick question. The whole point of the foregoing discussion about the difference between the formal and informal face of any organisation was to illustrate that you cannot engage with this informal side through conventional means. There is little point in developing a 'communities of practice strategy' that involves holding meetings, allocating tasks, enrolling users, and writing briefing papers. Many organisations are resistant to promoting informal networks because they can seem like avenues for staff to goof off. However, 'gossip in the workplace, often considered wasted time, is the way the company's knowledge network updates itself' (Davenport and Prusak, 1998:38). Formal networks go stale almost as soon as they are established, but informal networks, precisely because they are dynamic, never do.

In other words, do not attempt to formalise your communities of practice (a surprisingly common response). Instead, give them the time and space they need, to do what they do well. The aim is to create an organisation with structured informality, not informal structures. Stewart talks about how organisations need to 'fertilise the ground but keep away from the tending.' If you give the communities too many resources, this will increase the pressure on them for outputs and defeat the whole point. The best way to fertilise the ground for communities of practice is to recognise the important role they play in the organisation, and then provide members the time and space they need to come together. These requirements should be minimal – perhaps an intranet and the use of a conference room from time to time – but should pay substantial rewards.

COMMUNITIES OF PRACTICE AT WORK: THE FORD EXAMPLE

The knowledge management system at Ford Motor Company is built around communities of practice. Dar Wolford, whose job title of Manager of Best Practice Replication gives the game away, sees the system's role as capturing the best ideas from anywhere in Ford's global operations to create company-wide best practice. The communities of practice in this case are transnational, described by Wolford as 'people who do the same thing, wherever in the company they happen to be.' Ford has 19 such communities, where, for instance, 'everybody who does body work in any Ford plant world-wide belongs to the same community of practice ... ditto for vehicle painting, stamping, parts distribution, product design.' Business practice replication begins when a team or a person is proud of something they are doing. To leverage this 'pride', Ford has appointed a 'Focal Person' in each of its plants that these people can take their ideas and practices to. The focal person then enters this idea into a software program that runs on the company's intranet. Thus, this idea is automatically shared with Ford's 38 other assembly plants. Teams at those plants review the new ideas on a regular basis and decide whether to trial them in their own plants. If a plant does adopt the new practice, a projection of the cost savings involved is made and this is recorded. This can then be compared with the actual savings achieved over a period of six or twelve months. All this information is then assimilated into a summary of the new practice and hosted on the intranet (see Gordon, 1999).

You Get What You Reward

One obvious way to develop knowledge stocks (through encouraging staff to use more of what they know, or motivating them to learn new things) is simply to reward staff for their knowledge contributions. It may have been enough for (Ralph Waldo) Emerson that 'the reward of a thing well done is to have done it', but virtually everyone else will tell you that 'you get what you reward'. In any organisation that takes knowledge management seriously, knowledge creation and sharing need to become behaviours that are linked to remuneration. In the words of

Thomas Davenport and John Beck: 'In a world in which speed, knowledge, and creativity are vital, doesn't it seem odd that most of us are still paid for how long we take to complete a job or how much the deliverable weighs?' (2001:29).

Rewarding knowledge workers requires creativity. For instance, it is no accident that employee stock ownership has grown alongside the knowledge economy (or that such options are more prevalent in knowledge-intensive businesses than in traditional companies). As well as equity, companies are increasingly using incentive-pay plans and flexible working arrangements to reward their knowledge workers. Things which were once limited to the world of professional sports — such as signing bonuses — or to the world of academia — such as sabbaticals — are becoming increasingly common in knowledge-intensive organisations.

Consider the example of Microsoft: the average software employee was paid a salary of US$70,000 in 2000, but exercised stock options brought the average package closer to US$400,000 (Hood, 2000). As Microsoft's CFO put it, 'employee ownership is a profound example of how the information age has changed the nature of the corporation' (in Stewart, 1999:104). Indeed, Microsoft's motivation for taking the company public in 1986 was not to raise capital (the traditional reason for a share float) but to monetise the value of their employee ownership programme. In other words, 'forming a corporation and taking it public gave [Microsoft's] employees a financial incentive to keep their assets working for Microsoft, rather than take them elsewhere' (Stewart, 1999:105). In the words of *The Economist*: 'Involvement breeds loyalty' (8 December 2001:60).

BOTTOMING OUT AT THE BOTTOM OF THE WORLD?

The increasingly competitive market for skills means employers need to be more flexible, and work harder, to recruit and retain the knowledge-work stars. This is especially pertinent for New Zealand employers because our economy 'pays knowledge economy workers relatively poorly compared to most knowledge-driven economies' (ITAG, 1999:23). The results are inevitable: well-educated people in New Zealand are twice as likely to emigrate as their counterparts in the United States. Indeed, New Zealand's ability to retain skilled workers is on a par with that of countries like China and Venezuela. Even the Czech Republic and Thailand do a better job of retaining their knowledge graduates than we do (all ITAG, 1999:24). Given that it is unlikely New Zealand will ever be able to match the size of overseas salaries, local employers need to put together creative packages that make the most of the local advantages. What price sailing on the Waitemata, lunches at the Viaduct, winters in Wanaka, and a safe place to raise the kids?

The challenge facing many organisations is not how they should reward staff for creating and sharing knowledge, but that their existing payment-and-reward systems don't. This gives rise to two challenges. The major challenge is that a knowledge management initiative will not get very far if – however actively you champion knowledge sharing – the existing remuneration system rewards knowledge hoarding and individual successes (and, equally, penalises staff for making mistakes). The minor challenge is how to integrate or append rewards for knowledge creating and sharing behaviours to an existing, embedded, reward system. Our solution to this challenge is simple: why not introduce regular knowledge-sharing awards? This way, the rewards for knowledge creation and sharing can work in tandem with the existing remuneration system. Given the inevitable rhetoric about 'how valuable knowledge is', it is essential that these 'awards' are more than merely gimmicks. You need to give something away that staff will want to strive for. And you need to make a big deal about the awards – thus creating the opportunity to use the award ceremony to promote, and educate staff about, knowledge management. As Melisse Rumizen suggests, 'you need to create new heroes' (2002:180) out of your knowledge role-models.

Increasing Knowledge Flows
One day with a great teacher is better than a thousand days' study.
– CHINESE PROVERB

Having the knowledge stocks in your organisation sorted will reap few benefits if you do not also find ways to ensure that knowledge flows where it is needed in the organisation. We think whoever chose the label 'flow' picked the perfect metaphor. In contrast to the gentle flow sought, many organisations overwhelm their staff with a flood of information (too much information, too quickly), many send their staff on a treasure hunt in search of the knowledge they need (too hard to find), and still others make staff wrestle the knowledge from its holder (too much hoarding).

How to create knowledge flows (and not floods or treasure hunts or wrestling matches) is all about enabling staff to easily find the useful information, bottle it, and pass it around. It is about **knowledge transfer**.

It will come as no surprise that the best way to do this is to create systems that enable (and allow) staff to talk and listen to each other. It will be no surprise because this is already the way that most of us share knowledge in our organisations: people ask those in the office down the hall how they put together a budget request or create an e-mail user group. However, this informal way of sharing knowledge is both local and fragmentary ('satisficing' rather than optimising, in the language of economists). We ask the most conveniently located person, or the one with whom we get along best, rather than seeking out the best person in the organisation. To improve the sharing and transfer of knowledge, organisations should consider creating knowledge maps, talk spaces or a smart office layout, dedicated knowledge-sharing events, a common language, knowledge leaders, a change in culture – and even room for tension.

Knowledge Maps

A knowledge map shows where knowledge resides in the organisation. Also known as the knowledge management 'Yellow Pages', it is a detailed directory of who knows what, where. Chapter six will have a great deal more to say about knowledge maps and how to compile them.

Talk Spaces

Talk spaces can be as simple as the areas around the water-cooler or coffee pot, or as sophisticated as dedicated 'chill out' rooms. The point of such spaces is that they provide opportunities for staff to talk with one another in an informal setting. Although much office gossip is not about work, a great deal of what staff talk about is. The conversations staff have with one another are 'the way knowledge workers discover what they know, share it with their colleagues, and in the process create new knowledge for the organization' (Davenport and Prusak, 1998:90). What kind of space you create, and how you encourage staff to use it, has to fit with the broader existing workplace culture. Clear Communications, for instance, has 'chill zones' replete with comfortable sofas, TVs and DVD players, and furnishings chosen by the staff (Jayne, 2001b). By contrast, in Japan, some corporations have dedicated 'talk rooms' where staff are compelled to spend a portion of each day, usually talking to someone new.

A FULL HOUSE, AND FLUSH (WITH KNOWLEDGE)

There is a famous story of how Xerox Parc once hired an anthropologist to study the way technical representatives on Xerox's helpdesk team worked together. He discovered the key was that, while eating, playing cards, and engaging in what might otherwise seem like idle gossip, the reps talked about work continuously. 'They pose questions, raise problems, offer solutions, construct answers, laugh at mistakes and discuss changes in their work, the machines, and customer relations. Both directly and indirectly they keep one another up to date with what they know, what they have learned, and what they are doing.' (Calder, 2001:B4).

Smart Office Layout

In some organisations, the need for 'talk zones' is obviated by the layout of the office. One organisation we work with discovered they didn't need more water-coolers or sofas because they were a small team in an open-plan office, with a culture that encouraged mingling. The larger point is that good office design can contribute to an effective learning environment. As we have seen, the first response many people have to a novel problem is to ask the person closest to them what they should do. Why not simply rearrange the seating to ensure staff sit closest to the people who are likely to help them most in the future?

Dedicated Knowledge-Sharing Events

Think about organising a 'knowledge fair' or some kind of open forum where staff can share their knowledge. The term 'knowledge fair' sounds outrageous but really just means any opportunity for staff to meet and talk to other staff about their work. These can be semi-serious 'trade shows' (Stephen Denning talks about one such 'fair' organised in the atrium of the World Bank building [2001:138-140]) or they can be as simple as a corporate picnic. It is about creating the opportunity for exchange between people who never get to meet during the course of their daily work. Remember, too, that less structure is always better for these events in terms of knowledge sharing. Remaining loosely structured allows participants to 'pull' the kind of knowledge they want, building their own itineraries to meet their own needs.

Common Language

A major factor in the success of any knowledge transfer project is having a common language with which members of staff from throughout the organisation (and from different disciplinary backgrounds) can communicate with each another. Without one, any attempts at knowledge sharing will, in Kenneth Boulding's memorable phrase, 'grind to a stop in an assemblage of walled-in hermits, each mumbling to himself words in a private language that only he [sic] can understand'

(1956:198). Start with the creation of a glossary and thesaurus. These recognise that different disciplines have different languages, and cannot learn from each other until the knowledge has been translated into their own words.

Knowledge Leaders

No knowledge management initiative will work without someone senior in the organisation taking responsibility for it. This is the person who marshals the resources, champions the logic of knowledge-sharing, enrols the participation of staff, and models knowledge-sharing behaviours. Melissie Rumizen reminds us that 'leaders are always on display ... they must talk the talk and walk the walk because someone is always watching' (2002:178). What leaders do, how they spend their time, how they allocate their resources, matters.

A Change in Culture

The big one! We have talked about how driving knowledge sharing to the heart of any organisation relies on the staff being willing to share their knowledge and experiences (and open to learning from the knowledge and experience of others). Because genuine sharing is always voluntary, the challenge is to create a culture where people are eager to share their knowledge. Yet make no mistake, even rudimentary knowledge-management efforts require a requisite shift in culture. To take one obvious example, the creation of a knowledge map will be of no use in an organisation that is resistant to knowledge sharing. Knowing that Helen in marketing is an expert in dealing with e-commerce in Asia will be no use to anyone if she is not motivated to share her experiences with others.

The easiest way to demonstrate to staff that you are serious about knowledge sharing is to remove the barriers to the free flow of knowledge. This means circumventing (and even scrapping) the rules and procedures that suffocate the generation of new ideas. For instance, at Hewlett Packard the new culture was reflected in a directive that information users should have access to any data that would help them perform their jobs, unless specifically limited by management. The emphasis shifted to managers having to justify why they limited access to that knowledge, rather than end users having to justify their need for it. Moreover, the new culture was also reflected in a revised corporate structure, within which scientists and engineers could advance their careers by becoming senior exponents of their disciplines without shifting into management. The reorganisation of the business around functions enabled specialists to thrive (and, hence, be rewarded for their specialist contributions).

To assess how seriously your organisation takes the question of knowledge sharing, ask yourself 'When do staff do the reading needed to keep them abreast of developments in the industry or their discipline?' Or try these more specific questions: how would someone seen reading at their desk be viewed in your organisation? What if a senior manager went to talk to them but was told 'Can you come back later, I'm in the middle of some interesting reading here'? Yet any company which 'claims to value knowledge but discourages reading and talking on company time sends mixed messages' (Davenport and Prusak, 1998:93). Indeed, the amount of 'slack' time provided to staff for learning and thinking may be one of the best metrics for a firm's commitment to becoming a knowledge-centred organisation.

THE CULTURE OF KNOWLEDGE TRANSFER

Thomas Davenport and Larry Prusak (1998) provide the following list of the most common barriers to smooth knowledge flows, and suggestions for overcoming them:

Lack of trust	Build relationships and trust through face-to-face meetings
Different cultures, vocabularies, and frames of reference	Create common ground through glossaries, thesauri, education, discussions, teaming, and job rotation
Lack of time and meeting places (narrow idea of productive work)	Establish times and places for knowledge transfers (fairs, talk rooms, water-coolers)
Status and rewards going to knowledge owners	Evaluate performance and provide incentives based on sharing
Lack of absorptive capacity in recipients	Educate employees for flexibility; provide time and resources for learning; hire staff who are open to learning
Belief that experts know best, and 'not invented here' problem	Encourage the notion that the quality of the idea is much more important than its source
Intolerance for mistakes or need for help	Accept and reward creative errors and collaboration; no loss of status for not knowing everything

Create Room for Tension

Learning and innovative solutions often occur when people are made to stretch their thinking in novel ways. One way to do this — alternatively called 'fusion', 'creative abrasion', or 'creative tension' — is to bring staff from different parts of the organisation together to work on the same problem. The different skills, ideas, and values should combine to create innovative solutions. Where managed well, this abrasion overcomes path-dependent thinking and creates the space for synergies to occur. Another way to achieve creative tension is to hire people from different disciplines or with different experiences and bring them together under the same roof.

The label 'creative abrasion' reminds us that no-one can be creative in the face of too much abrasion, and signals the need for such processes to be managed well. This means creating rules about how the groups will function, in spite of the fact that: 'People often feel a bit foolish creating rules about how they will work together ... surely, the thinking goes, we are all adults and have years of experience in dealing with group dynamics' (Leonard and Straus, 1998:124). But this is the problem, the old ways are not creative ways. As the old saying has it: 'If you do what you've always done, you'll get what you've always got.' Or, in the words of Phyllis Diller: 'Never go to bed mad. Stay up and fight.'

'THAT'S EXACTLY WHAT I'D DO ...'

If you want an innovative organization, you need to hire, work with, and promote people who make you uncomfortable. You need to understand your own preferences so that you can complement your weaknesses and exploit your strengths (Leonard and Straus, 1998:117). If you have a problem and you go to someone who is on the same wavelength as you, you may get encouragement but you are unlikely to get the spark of a new idea.

The Knowledge Marketplace

A friend in the marketplace is better than money in the chest.
– WEST AFRICAN PROVERB

One further way we can conceptualise how knowledge stocks and flows operate (and how to maximise them both) is through the notion of the knowledge marketplace that exists inside an organisation. As with all markets, knowledge markets involve people looking for the knowledge they need (buyers), people with that knowledge (sellers), and the intermediaries who bring them together (brokers). Clearly, these roles are not mutually exclusive or fixed – someone may play all three roles in the same day and even simultaneously. But what is useful about the notion of the knowledge market is that it focuses attention on the 'currency' used to buy and sell knowledge. When you bring in a consultant, the fee is negotiated beforehand and is tied to a number of milestones and outcomes. Yet if we work in the same organisation and you come to me with a question or problem, how do I get 'paid' for sharing my knowledge with you?

The answer, according to Davenport and Prusak (1998) and others, is remarkably simple. **This market runs on reciprocity.** It's what Tom Wolfe, in *The Bonfire of the Vanities*, labelled 'the favo[u]r bank' (Wolfe, 1990). This is the idea that I will share my knowledge with you because you – or someone you know – will have access to the knowledge I may need in the future. This, put simply, is what 'social exchange theory' explains.

THE THEORY OF SOCIAL EXCHANGE

The theory of social exchange argues that the actions of individuals are motivated by the return that these actions are expected to bring. People engage in an activity because of the rewards they hope to reap, but all activities include certain costs, and people attempt to keep the costs below the rewards they expect to receive (Dillman, 1978). The anthropological view on social exchange is that any exchange involves a measure of obligation, and that social order is an effect of the underlying ritual and symbolic nature of the thing exchanged. Where the exchange breaks down (and the obligation of reciprocity is not fulfilled), conflict and disorder occur (Marshall, 1994).

The notion of reciprocity equates with the idea of rational action (and actors) in 'real' markets. But as with all markets, there is more going on in the knowledge market than simple rational action. In the same way that many consumers pursue status for wholly irrational reasons, knowledge markets also function thanks to some participants wanting to show off their riches. Every knowledge market will have people who share their knowledge simply because they want others to see them as knowledgeable people with valuable expertise. People will thus share their knowledge in order to enhance their reputations in the workplace. Finally, in the same way that in 'real' markets some people give away some of their wealth to charity (or donate their time as volunteers) out of sheer altruism, there will always be those in knowledge markets who share their knowledge freely. These knowledge 'sellers' give away their expertise because they like the person who is doing the 'buying' and see the 'sale' as for the good of the company, or for other selfless reasons. Mentoring is a common form of knowledge sharing based on altruism.

So now we know what fuels the market (reciprocity, status seeking, and altruism), we can turn our attention to the critical conditions needed for the market to function. Those are conditions which provide, in Francis Fukuyama's memorable phrase, 'the social virtues' which underpin 'the creation of prosperity' (Fukuyama, 1996). **The virtue which most obviously underpins any market is trust.** Fukuyama talks about 'the improbable power of trust' in making any kind of market work (*Ibid.*), and knowledge markets are no different. Davenport and Prusak are unequivocal:

> **Without trust, knowledge management initiatives will fail, regardless of how thoroughly they are supported by technology and rhetoric and even if the survival of the organization depends on effective knowledge transfer (Davenport and Prusak, 1998:34).**

But how do you *establish* a culture of trust? Fukuyama's argument about cultural (and religious) traditions is an interesting one at the societal level, but what happens if you want to create a new, high-trust, environment in the workplace? Again, Davenport and Prusak provide the way ahead. They make the following three suggestions:

- Trust must be visible. Staff must see people get credit for knowledge sharing. This strengthens reciprocity.
- Trust must be ubiquitous. The culture must include everyone or it will include no-one.
- Trustworthiness must start at the top. Trust flows downward through organisations. Management needs to set examples.

And nothing builds trust like personal contact. Consequently, face-to-face meetings are essential for an organisation building a knowledge culture. There is nothing 'virtual' about trust or its construction.

The knowledge market needs an environment of trust if it is to flourish. But beyond trust, the market also requires a number of signals in order to function. These signals indicate where knowledge *actually* resides in the organisation and how others can gain access to it. Such signals can be formal (such as job title, education, and experience) or informal (such as word-of-mouth endorsements). In general, the informal signals provide the more accurate guide to where knowledge resides in any organisation. Again, we talk much more about how to 'chart' these informal signals to create a knowledge map from the 'bottom up' in the next chapter.

Beyond Merely Flowing: Getting Staff to Use Knowledge

Skill comes so slow, and life so fast doth fly
We learn so little and forget so much.
- JOHN DAVIES (1599)

The final idea introduced in this chapter is that it is not enough to ensure that your organisation has the right knowledge stocks and that this knowledge is flowing to the places in the organisation where it is needed. What matters is that staff use that knowledge to work smarter. To put this another way, knowledge management is ultimately about learning.

Charles Handy provides the following simple model of learning:

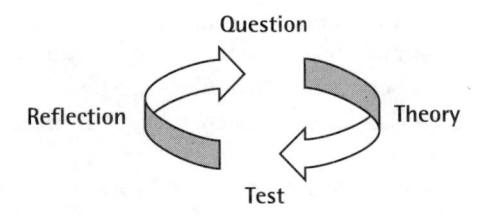

He uses the idea of a wheel to describe learning because one set of questions, once answered and reflected upon, leads to another set. Handy calls it 'life's special treadmill' because if you 'step off it you ossify' (Handy, 1990:46). For Handy, 'learning is discovery, and discovery only works when you are looking.' So the ultimate fuel for this learning wheel is curiosity. When faced with a problem, we first need to be motivated to think about how to solve it (or else, as an old *Peanuts* cartoon put it, 'there is no problem big enough that it cannot be run away from'). With that motivation in place, we then look for ideas about how to solve the problem – and this is where knowledge sharing plays such an important role. Armed with some good ideas, we then apply and test those until we are happy the problem is solved. The real learning occurs at the next stage, the one where we *reflect* on why those ideas worked, what was learned, and, in many cases, how those ideas could be improved in future. The 'test–reflection' relationship is crucial because, to quote Handy again:

> Learning is *not* finding out what other people already know, but is solving our own problems for our own purposes, by questioning, thinking, and testing until the solution is a new part of our life (1990:50).

Or, as we might say in knowledge management, until we internalise the knowledge used (that is, have converted the explicit knowledge of others into our own tacit knowledge). The value of Handy's model is that it is clear that learning is more than simply problem-solving.

Chris Argyris (1998) uses the notions of 'single-loop' and 'double-loop' thinking to illustrate a similar point. Single-loop thinking is akin to path dependency – with a certain problem eliciting a certain solution. Double-loop thinking involves reflecting on the solutions used, and questioning whether there are other solutions that could be tried. Argyris uses the analogy of a thermostat, one that automatically turns on the heat when the temperature in a room drops below some threshold. The thermostat is involved in single-loop thinking, and is heavily path dependent (this problem requires this solution, and receives it every time). By contrast, a thermostat capable of double-loop thinking would ask 'Why am I set at this particular threshold?' and then explore whether there were other thresholds that might more economically or efficiently heat the room.

How people learn is a complex issue that has a material bearing on successful knowledge-management. The most common taxonomy of different learning styles identifies:

- **Visual learners:** people who learn best from visual displays, including: diagrams, illustrated textbooks, overhead transparencies, videos, flipcharts and hand-outs. During a lesson, visual learners often prefer to take detailed notes to absorb the information.
- **Auditory learners:** people who learn best through verbal lectures, discussions, talking things through and listening to what others have to say. Auditory learners interpret the underlying meanings of speech through listening to tone of voice, pitch,

speed and other nuances. Written information may have little meaning until it is heard. These learners often benefit from reading text aloud and using a tape recorder.
- **Tactile/kinaesthetic learners:** people who learn best through a hands-on approach, actively exploring the content of the lesson. They may find it hard to sit still for long periods and need activity and exploration (http://www.ldpride.net/learningstyles.MI.htm).

'Learning styles' are also intimately tied to the notion of 'multiple intelligences'. Conceived by Howard Gardner (1983), this idea tells us that intellectual ability comes in a number of different varieties. The seven commonly identified are:

- visual/spatial intelligence: ability to perceive the visual
- verbal/linguistic intelligence: ability to use words and language
- logical/mathematical intelligence: ability to use reason, logic and numbers
- bodily/kinaesthetic intelligence: ability to control body movements and handle objects skilfully
- interpersonal intelligence: ability to relate to, and understand, others
- intrapersonal intelligence: ability to self-reflect and be aware of one's inner state of being
- musical/rhythmic intelligence: ability to produce and appreciate music.

MULTIPLE INTELLIGENCES AND KNOWLEDGE MANAGEMENT SKILLS

Visual/spatial intelligence skills: puzzle building, reading, writing, understanding charts and graphs, having a good sense of direction, creating visual metaphors and analogies, manipulating images, constructing, fixing, designing practical objects, interpreting visual images

Verbal/linguistic intelligence skills: listening, speaking, writing, storytelling, explaining, teaching, using humour, understanding the syntax and meaning of words, remembering information, convincing someone of your point of view

Logical/mathematical intelligence skills: problem-solving, classifying and categorising information, working with abstract concepts to figure out relationships among them, handling long chains of reasoning to make local progressions

Bodily/kinaesthetic intelligence skills: physical coordination, sports, hands-on experimentation, using body language, crafts, acting, miming, using your hands to create or build, expressing emotions through the body

Interpersonal intelligence skills: listening, using empathy, understanding others, counselling, cooperating with groups, communicating both verbally and non-verbally, building trust, resolving conflict peacefully, establishing positive relations with other people

Intrapersonal intelligence skills: recognising your own strengths and weaknesses, reflecting on and analysing yourself, evaluating your thinking patterns, reasoning with yourself, understanding your role in relationship to others

Musical/rhythmic intelligence skills: singing, whistling, playing musical instruments, recognising tonal patterns, composing music, remembering melodies, understanding the structure and rhythm of music

---

We have introduced the notions of learning styles and multiple intelligences because they make it clear that different people prefer to learn in very different ways. And if knowledge management is ultimately about learning, then what is required is a knowledge management strategy that takes these different styles into consideration. Our suggestion is that organisations use competency maps (and performance reviews, etc.) to highlight the preferred learning styles of staff. Although it is likely that staff will not be clear about what kinds of learners they are, there are any number of inventory questionnaires that can be used to help assess their most effective learning styles (see for example www.creativelearningcentre.com). Doing so will help maximise the success of their learning. Without such insight, managers tend to manage their staff the way they themselves would like to be managed. Leonard and Straus are clear: 'Don't treat people the way you want to be treated. Tailor communications to the receiver instead of the sender ... Information must be delivered in the preferred 'language' of the recipient if it is to be received at all' (1998:118).

Note, too, that the idea of different learning styles has important implications for how information is presented (and learning supported) by the in-house computer system. What organisations need to aim for is not a system that supports a generic model of 'learning' (and communication) but one that can be adapted by users to their own style and needs. Remember what we said in chapter four about computers being useful only to the extent that they support learning.

A Victim of Their Success?

On the question of learning, there are three more important points we should make. The first is that those staff who you might assume would be best at learning (that is, the professionals in key leadership roles) may actually be among the very worst at it. Why this is the case goes back to Chris Argyris's notion of single- and double-loop learning. Professionals are often very good at single-loop learning ('This kind of problem requires that kind of solution') but poor at double-loop learning ('Why do we do it this way?') precisely because the single-loop trip will have proved so successful in the past. Argyris writes: 'Because many professionals are almost always successful at what they do, they rarely experience failure. And because they have rarely failed, they have never learned how to learn from failure' (Argyris, 1998:83).

Indeed, when their tried-and-true, single-loop, solutions fail they are more likely to become defensive and look for others to blame rather than search for novel solutions. 'In short, their ability to learn shuts down precisely at the moment they need it most' (Argyris, 1998:83). What is needed is to teach these people how to deal with 'failure', how to respond to it, and how to learn from it. The broader need here is to create an organisational culture where it is acceptable to make mistakes.

The second point is that it is not only the mature professional workers who may have trouble learning. We have worked with a professional services firm that had a policy of recruiting only the highest-achieving and most ambitious graduates. Curiously, many of these graduates also proved poor at learning – because they were so used to being the smartest person they knew. This was reflected in a reluctance to learn from others or from the previous experience of the organisation. These graduates started from the implicit assumption, 'I bet I can come up with something better than anything those other people created.' To these people, knowledge was not just 'power' but a key part of their identity.

The third point deals with how you get the mature professional staff (and the young hotshots) to think creatively. The professional training of these staff has not nurtured creativity but rewarded meticulousness. And there are certainly moments when this is appropriate. After all, there is little call for accountants to account creatively or for pilots to fly creatively. The challenge for managers is to prepare professionals to be able to think creatively when circumstances require (such as when faced with novel problems, emergencies, etc.)

Amid all this talk about learning we need to reiterate that there is no learning without making mistakes. This raises important questions about how your own organisation responds to those who make mistakes. Best practice here belongs to a (probably apocryphal) story told to us by one of our MBA students. It involves a manager in a company who took a gamble on a new marketing strategy. Unfortunately, it did not turn out well, and the organisation took a bath to the tune of several hundred thousand dollars. When another manager asked the CEO when he was going to fire the miscreant, the CEO replied: 'Fire him? Why would I want to fire him? I just spent half-a-million bucks on his education.'

Successful Knowledge Management: A Quick Summary

A great many people think they are thinking when they are merely rearranging their prejudices.
– WILLIAM JAMES

This chapter has argued for three simple points:

- Successful knowledge management is all about learning (learning how to do our jobs better, faster, smarter).
- This is achieved by having the right knowledge stocks in place, and making sure that knowledge flows to the places in the organisation where it is needed.
- The knowledge stocks and flows rely on having (i) the right knowledge streams and sources feeding in to the organisation; (ii) the right technology to store and communicate that knowledge; and (iii) the right workplace culture so that staff are motivated to make use of that knowledge.

Other chapters have emphasised how knowledge management goals need to be aligned with the organisation's broader strategic goals. Clearly, what staff learn needs to be things that ultimately enable the organisation to develop in the way desired. This chapter has emphasised the role that culture plays in successful knowledge management – that 'learning' (and, hence, knowledge-creating and knowledge-sharing behaviour) is a cultural phenomenon. Creating an effective knowledge management culture therefore relies on:

- acknowledging the role that 'informal' structures play in workplace learning;
- rewarding staff for learning, sharing knowledge, or creating knowledge – and removing the disincentives for them to exhibit those behaviours;

- creating the time and space for staff to create knowledge, share knowledge, and learn;
- having senior staff lead and model knowledge-creating and knowledge-sharing behaviours;
- introducing a measure of creative tension to challenge staff to think in novel ways; and
- allowing people to make mistakes.

Although writing this list was easy enough, we hope this chapter has left no-one in any doubt about how far-reaching the cultural changes required to achieve successful knowledge management really are. This is why we have insisted that any knowledge management project is also fundamentally a change management project. In the next chapter, we talk about the best place to get started with those changes.

chapter six

Knowledge Management in Action

The important thing when you are going to do something brave is to have someone on hand to witness it.
– MICHAEL HOWARD

The Yellow Brick Road

Whenever we teach about knowledge management, or talk about it at conferences or seminars, the question we are inevitably asked goes something along the lines of: 'That's all very interesting, but how do I actually get started?' As we have emphasised throughout this book, our experiences make it clear to us that there is no simple recipe for successful knowledge management. However, if we strain that recipe/cooking metaphor to breaking point, it is also clear that, although there may be no easy-to-follow recipe for how to manage knowledge, there are certainly some important pointers on what ingredients to use, and even how to prepare them.

The model we use is a simple step-wise one that breaks the knowledge management process down into a number of important phases:

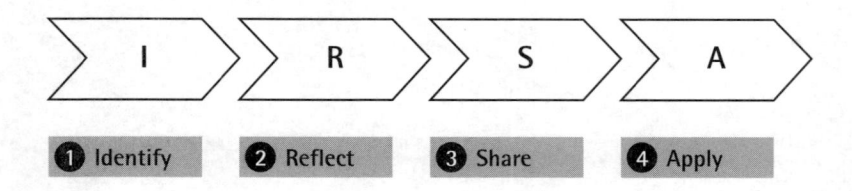

> I   >   R   >   S   >   A   >

❶ Identify   **❷ Reflect**   **❸ Share**   **❹ Apply**

Hence, we believe, the key to successful knowledge management is creating a strategy that enables you to carry out each phase of the process.

1. IDENTIFY **where the key knowledge exists in your organisation.** Knowledge management starts by identifying what you already know. This includes the knowledge which resides (i) in the minds of your staff, (ii) in reports stored in the corporate library or dusty office corners, (iii) in data sets held throughout the organisation, or (iv) among your regular suppliers and customers. The genesis for any knowledge management strategy is to be clear about where you are able to start.
2. REFLECT **on what your organisation knows.** Once you have identified where the existing knowledge resides in your organisation, the next step is to take stock of that knowledge. What is it that you know? How useful is that knowledge? Reflecting on what you know provides the opportunity for (i) turning your staff's tacit knowledge into explicit knowledge and, where appropriate, (ii) summarising the existing knowledge into a form that can be easily shared with others. This also enables your organisation to identify the gaps in the existing knowledge stock and, hence, focus future knowledge-gathering efforts. As an added bonus, reflecting on what it is that your organisation knows provides a powerful mechanism for generating suggestions about how things might be done differently. In this regard, the 'reflection' phase is often one that can pay immediate dividends.
3. SHARE **that knowledge with whoever needs to know it.** A critical component of knowledge management is creating a system that ensures knowledge is shared with those who need it. The aim is to make the knowledge that exists *anywhere* in your organisation available *everywhere* it is needed in the organisation. Consequently, once your knowledge stock has been identified and codified, the emphasis shifts to sharing that knowledge in the most effective way possible.
4. APPLY **that knowledge to improve the way your organisation performs.** As we have emphasised, knowledge management is all about knowledge in action. The single reason organisations embark on a knowledge management strategy is to improve the way they perform (in the broadest possible sense). Hence, the ultimate goal of identifying, reflecting upon, and sharing what an organisation knows is to apply that knowledge. Where such knowledge is demonstrated to offer improved performance, organisations will then need to go beyond merely 'applying' it,

and create systems that embed that knowledge into their normal operating procedures (and, hence, turn that knowledge into structural capital).

For obvious reasons, we call this the I–R–S–A approach. We will discuss what is involved in each of these steps in more detail throughout this chapter, but here it is important to note that an obvious strength of the I–R–S–A approach is that it reflects a commonsense logic about how an organisation can work through developing its own knowledge management strategy. Before an organisation can go about applying its best insights, it first has to find a way to share those successfully among its staff. Before it can share its knowledge, the organisation needs to be clear about the value of what it knows – carefully assessing and weighing those insights, checking for gaps, and making sure it couches that knowledge in a language accessible to everyone. Before it can assess the value of what it knows, the organisation needs to be clear about what exactly it does know. A diagrammatic overview of this process would look like this:

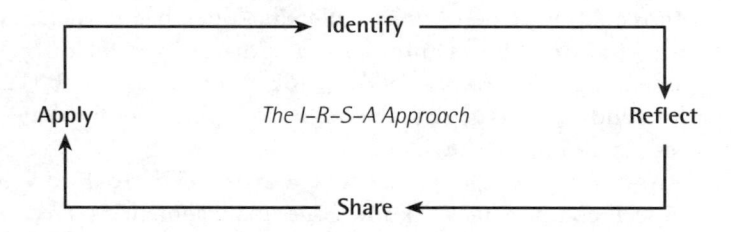

```
          ──────▶ Identify ──────┐
          │                       │
          │                       ▼
  Apply       The I-R-S-A Approach    Reflect
    ▲                              │
    │                              │
    └────────── Share ◀────────────┘
```

Looking After the Goose That Lays the Golden Eggs

The past is but the beginning of a beginning, and all that is and has been is but the twilight of the dawn.
– H G WELLS

The I–R–S–A model is drawn as a cycle to underscore the point that **knowledge management is a process**. Once an organisation has identified its existing knowledge, reflected on that, shared it among the relevant staff, and then applied it, it will inevitably have learned new things (indeed, by definition, the I–R–S–A process is one of discovery, meaning organisations will know more at the end than they did at the outset). As our colleague Trevor Williamson likes to say, 'You can never learn less.' However, although the process should create a virtuous cycle, some organisations do become distracted by the many lessons learned (and suggestions made) during the initial iteration of the process. In this regard, these organisations shift their attention and energies to the golden eggs supplied by the process and away from the goose that laid them. In doing so, the emphasis shifts from the ongoing strategic advantage that a successful knowledge-management strategy can provide and towards short-term operational gains. This is perhaps easier to see with the help of a diagram:

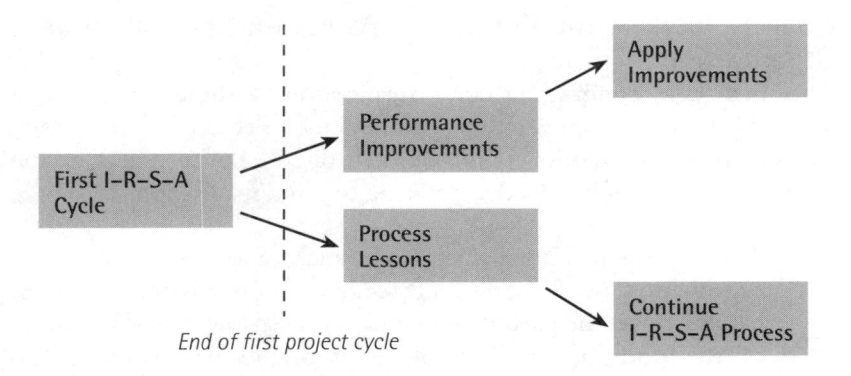

End of first project cycle

In this diagram, we can track an organisation embarking on the I–R–S–A approach to knowledge management. In normal circumstances, it can be expected that this approach will provide the organisation with both a treasure trove of ideas about how to work smarter ('Performance Improvements' in the above diagram) and a series of lessons about how best to engage staff to continue to elicit such ideas ('Process Lessons'). Consequently, at the end of the first I–R–S–A cycle, the challenge is to find a way to apply those ideas and fine-tune the process according to the specific demands of the organisation's culture. Another way to say this is simply: **knowledge management is a verb, not a noun.**

KNOWLEDGE MANAGEMENT

Step One: Identify

Seek, and ye shall find.
– MATTHEW, 7:7

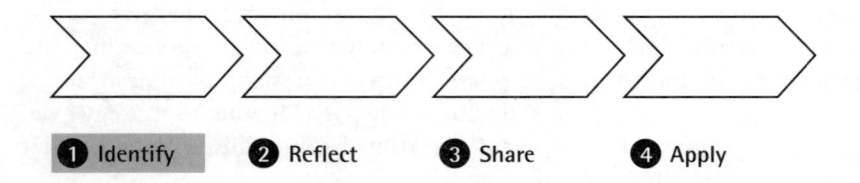

① Identify   ② Reflect   ③ Share   ④ Apply

Goal: To Identify the Knowledge Assets that Exist in Your Organisation

The first task confronting any organisation wishing to create a knowledge management strategy is to identify what knowledge already exists and where it resides. At this point, it often helps to reflect on the common sources of knowledge available to any organisation.

- The collected knowledge, experience, and creativity of an organisation's staff: commonly called an organisation's **human capital**, this is the part of an organisation's memory that walks out of the door at the end of the working day. Because this knowledge and experience tends to reside in the memories of staff rather than in policy manuals or briefing papers, the challenge here is how to turn **tacit knowledge** into explicit knowledge.
- The knowledge already captured in an organisation's document records, its databases, and filing cabinets: this might include procedure manuals, policy documents, market research reports, notes from meetings, memos, or a thousand other different kinds of records. Where this knowledge is already embedded into how an organisation does things it is known as **structural capital**. However, in many organisations, there is often much relevant and timely information that has not been acknowledged or acted upon. Because, by its very nature, this knowledge tends to be **explicit**, the challenge is to find where it is stored in any organisation (as likely to be a dusty shelf in someone's office as with the corporate librarian) and to be able to assess its usefulness; and
- The collected knowledge, experience, and creativity of an organisation's key suppliers and customers: commonly called

customer and supplier capital, this broadens the focus beyond what is known within a particular organisation to include those who deal with it on a regular basis.

The aim in identifying these knowledge sources is not to then attempt to codify this knowledge in any exhaustive way (an impossible task, given that there is so much knowledge; it changes so quickly; and some of it is uncodifiable anyway) but rather to create a comprehensive map of where the knowledge in the organisation resides. The key to knowledge management is to **connect users with users, not users with instructions**.

Identifying the knowledge that resides in each of these areas presents different challenges, which require the use of distinct methods. Although the actual expression of such methods will differ from organisation to organisation, the following provides some clear ideas about how to get started identifying key knowledge assets.

1. Identifying Who Knows What, Where, In Your Organisation

The first step in creating a knowledge map for any organisation is to find out who the key knowledge holders are. This part of the knowledge map is often referred to as the 'Yellow Pages' and provides a directory of which staff know what, where. Every member of the staff already has a piece of that map in their head. Creating the organisation-wide map is simply a case of putting these pieces together. Note that the picture of organisational expertise created by the 'Yellow Pages' is likely to be quite different from what people's job descriptions will suggest. This simply reflects the fact that how your organisation *actually* functions is somewhat different from what the organisational charts and formal job descriptions suggest. The distinction between the formal version of any organisation and the informal reality is a key one for successful knowledge management.

The best way to generate the 'Yellow Pages' is from the bottom up, by talking to staff and asking them where they go when they have certain kinds of questions. For instance, a sales and marketing team may have someone in it everyone comes to with questions about e-commerce, even though that person's expertise in e-commerce has little to do with their formal job description. This bottom-up generation of the 'Yellow Pages' can be done through a staff survey, through a series of in-depth one-on-one interviews (better), or through a series of facilitated group workshops (better still). The key question to ask staff is 'Where do you go when you want to know about X?' Group situations (such as workshops) work best here because they provide an opportunity to confirm the veracity of someone's expertise. In research circles, this is known as 'triangulation of data sources'. It simply means that if a number of people, independently, tell you that Michael in the store is the person to talk to about organising air freight shipments at short notice, you can have some confidence that this is the case.

The 'Yellow Pages' sum to a knowledge map of the human capital within an organisation if done well. Ideally, generating the bottom-up picture would involve a 360-degree peer review. Because staff may well have knowledge they are not currently using, or haven't been asked for by others, a self-audit of their knowledge assets is also required. However, it is important not to use *only* self-audit techniques, because there are serious generational biases at work here (the young hotshot staff will tell you they know just about everything, or can certainly learn about it readily; the grey-hairs may play down their knowledge, or be more aware of the limitations to it).

The 'snowball' sampling method is also often useful here. As we have seen elsewhere, the people critical to the flow of knowledge around an organisation are not simply the knowledge holders (experts) but also the knowledge connectors (conduits). In any organisation, it is likely that staff will tell you something along the lines of 'I don't know who to go to when I have a question about HTML [or whatever], but I'd ask Susan because she'll know who to talk to.' The task of the project team at this point is to pursue the 'seams of expertise' identified this way, hence weaving networks of applied expertise together.

2. Identifying Existing Knowledge Repositories

In a perfect world, it would be a simple task to identify the knowledge repositories available in any organisation: someone, somewhere, would have a complete list of all the databases the organisation had access to, a complete list of the research reports and consultants' reports written since the beginning of time, and a complete record of the process manuals, policy documents, and minutes existing within the organisation. Of course, there would still be a need to synthesise, summarise, and assess these secondary sources, but it would be clear to the project team where to start. In the real world, this is rarely the case. Few organisations we have been involved with have had such a record. In those cases where such records were thought to exist, they have turned out to be partial, out of date, or biased in some systematic way or another (such as privileging reports carried out since a new CEO came on board). As with human capital, so with these potential sources of structural capital: most organisations simply do not know what they know. Thus it is common for different departments within large organisations to duplicate one another's research efforts or pursue projects separately that could have been completed productively through collaboration. (This explains why one of the real benefits of a healthy knowledge management culture is the reduction of duplication of such efforts.)

Identifying 'what sources exist where' involves asking staff about the documents, manuals, or databases they use on a regular basis, as well as what other sources they know about. Although this part of the process usually involves face-to-face interviews with some key staff (information technology managers, customer service managers, corporate librarians, etc.), the real value here comes from running a series of focus groups with staff, structured around different functional areas. For instance, a focus group might bring together all staff in a factory who work in Distribution and have them identify secondary sources they use that describe what they do; that process might offer pointers on how they can improve current practice.

Once the key knowledge holders in an organisation (see page 119) and the key secondary sources used by staff in particular functional areas have been identified, the first part of the knowledge map can be created. A simplified version of that map, for a particular function, would follow this kind of structure:

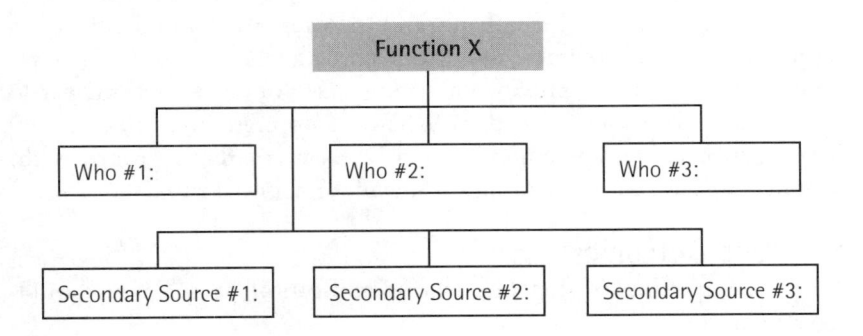

```
                      Function X
         ┌───────────────┼───────────────┐
       Who #1:         Who #2:         Who #3:
         ┌───────────────┼───────────────┐
  Secondary Source #1:  Secondary Source #2:  Secondary Source #3:
```

This kind of map provides a ready reference for the expertise that exists inside an organisation, both in terms of the 'living' knowledge of key experts and the 'stored' knowledge of key documentary sources. It provides an easy-to-follow guide about where the knowledge relevant to a particular function resides in an organisation. A second, equally important, dimension to the knowledge map is the evaluative component. This distils the ready reference chart into a series of frequently asked questions (FAQs) and provides users with a series of directions as to where to find answers. This part of the knowledge map is discussed fully under step three, 'Sharing'.

3. Identifying What Your Customers and Suppliers Know

In many regards this is the area of knowledge that makes many organisations most nervous. The question 'What do our suppliers and customers know about us that we should know?' is potentially a very contentious one. Moreover, there are often real concerns around (i) what customers and suppliers will make of an organisation seeking to change the nature of its traditional relationships with customers and suppliers, and (ii) how an organisation will react to criticism from those outside the organisation. Regardless, this is too important a source of knowledge for any organisation to overlook. For example, research carried out by James Quinn of Dartmouth College demonstrated that the customer–producer interface was the most productive source of innovations available to manufacturing organisations. According to Quinn's research, more than 50 per cent of all such innovation occurs at this interface (Quinn, et al., 1998).

The obvious way to pursue this knowledge is through a series of interviews with key informants (key contacts identified by your own staff in the workshops used to generate the in-house 'Yellow Pages'). It is important to brief the relevant customers and suppliers about the purpose of the exercise beforehand, and to ensure that confidentiality is respected. Indeed, in some cases, the need to guarantee confidentiality (and, hence, candour) provides a strong case for using a third-party organisation to gather these data. Where appropriate, the one-on-one interviews can be supplemented with a series of focus groups with suppliers or customers, focusing on specific functional issues.

Step One Outcomes

At the completion of step one (the identification phase), you should have identified

- who the key knowledge holders in your organisation are;
- who the key 'connectors' are;
- what the key secondary (that is, documentary and database) sources are; and
- what your customers and suppliers have to say about your organisation.

The products you should have completed are:

- a knowledge map, identifying key knowledge holders and the secondary sources available to them; and
- a summary of transcripts containing insights from your customers and suppliers.

Step Two: Reflect

What we need is a good five cent synthesis.
- SAUL BELLOW

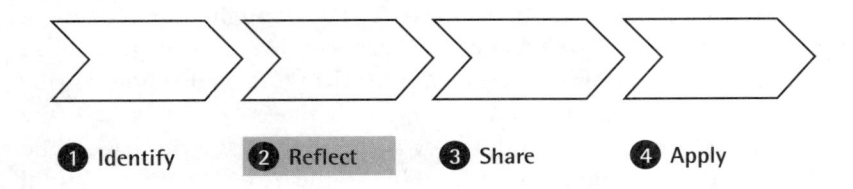

1 Identify **2** Reflect **3** Share **4** Apply

Goal: To Assess the Knowledge Assets that Exist in Your Organisation

Once an organisation has identified the range of knowledge sources available to it, the next challenge is to reflect on what is known. This is done to assess the value of that knowledge, and to see where the gaps in the existing knowledge set are (and, hence, where future knowledge-gathering efforts can be most productively directed). Reflecting on what your organisation knows provides a powerful mechanism for generating suggestions about how things could be done differently. In this regard, the 'reflection' phase is often one that can pay immediate dividends. At a minimum, this phase of the I–R–S–A process involves:

- converting the tacit knowledge that exists among staff into explicit knowledge that can be shared with others
- verifying the utility of that implicit knowledge
- summarising the documentary and database knowledge that exists throughout the organisation into a form that can be easily shared with others
- assessing the veracity and utility of existing documentary and database sources

- identifying the gaps in the collected existing knowledge and using these gaps to focus future knowledge-gathering efforts.

1. Turning Tacit Knowledge into Explicit Knowledge

One of the most difficult challenges in knowledge management is turning the tacit knowledge of your staff into explicit knowledge that can be shared with others. As we have seen, the concept of tacit knowledge draws our attention to the fact that people know more than they realise. In some cases, they know more than they can tell or explain to others. This is another powerful reason why successful knowledge management is about connecting users to users – the expert lathe operator may not be able to tell other operators how he knows the machine is running at an optimum speed but he is probably able to *show* them what it looks like. To demonstrate how fraught this process of making tacit knowledge explicit is, in chapter three we suggested you try writing out a set of instructions that explain to a novice how to ride a bicycle from scratch. It is notoriously difficult, no matter how many diagrams you may use. And yet, we presume that you have little difficulty actually riding the bike. This is the reason why successful knowledge management makes much use of mentoring schemes, 'buddying' relationships, and active induction programmes (see chapter seven). It is the same idea captured in the Confucian wisdom, 'I hear and I forget. I see and I remember. I do and I understand.'

There is no doubt that much tacit knowledge cannot be translated into any readily shared explicit knowledge. However, there is also plenty of tacit knowledge that can be. The challenge for any organisation is to distinguish the two. Our experience is that, in order to get 'experts' to tell you what they know, you first need to create the opportunity for them to reflect upon it. Ask someone who is good at their job why they do it the way they do, and there is a good chance they will say something like 'It's obvious' or 'It's common sense'. Of course, it is precisely because it is not obvious, nor commonsensical, that you have asked them in the first place. The way around this is to run a series of focus groups to bring experts from similar functions throughout an organisation together and – as a group – have them share their experiences and knowledge. In the group setting, various projection or visualisation techniques can be used to get staff to reflect on what they know. Useful questions often include:

- What do you know about your job now that you wished you had known when you started it?

- What is the most important thing about being good at your job?
- Why do you do it that way?
- How would you do your job in a workplace free of constraints?

A powerful way to capture tacit knowledge is through storytelling. Tools such as narratives, metaphors, and speaking figuratively enable staff, in the words of Ikujiro Nonaka, to 'put together what they know in new ways and begin to express what they know but cannot yet say' (1998:34). Lately most associated with the work of Stephen Denning, the programme director for knowledge management at the World Bank, storytelling has proved to be a most effective way of communicating tacit knowledge. Joseph Badaracco, a business ethics professor at Harvard Business School, attributes this efficacy to the fact that stories 'trigger things – pictures, thoughts and associations in [the listeners'] minds,' hence creating learning that is 'powerful and engaging' (Seglin, 2000).

2. Verifying the Utility of the Tacit Knowledge

For all the many benefits that tacit knowledge offers an organisation, it also has a number of potential downsides. Notably, tacit knowledge

- can be wrong
- is hard to change
- is hard to communicate.

It is only by making tacit knowledge explicit that these three problems can be overcome. Once out in the open, tacit knowledge can be examined, challenged, and changed. Fortunately, this is another strength of the focus group approach for making tacit knowledge explicit: by combining staff with similar areas of functional or operational expertise, the groups are able to provide a check on the quality of the knowledge expressed. Indeed, the group setting provides an environment where staff can learn about their own (often unquestioned) assumptions and about how others in similar positions do things differently. The focus groups used in the reflection stage provide an opportunity for staff to pause and think about their tacit knowledge, about how the different bits fit logically together, and how the ideas stack up against those held by their peers. Done well, this stage of the process not only provides a record of 'best practice' in an organisation (or, more likely, best *practices*) but also seeds the dissemination of that practice across key users.

The focus groups provide another important contribution to the knowledge management process, too – they provide an opportunity to ensure that you have identified all the key knowledge holders in the first stage of the process. By asking participants 'Is there anyone else we should talk to about X?' an organisation can ensure it has achieved saturation point around aspects of key expertise.

In the same way that (function-specific) focus groups are used to get knowledge holders to reflect on what they know, focus groups can also be held with customers and suppliers to test the veracity of the insights gathered through the key informant interviews. Where organisations are happy to do so, these groups can bring together customers and suppliers from different organisations to triangulate different aspects of customer/supplier service. In those organisations that are reluctant to combine suppliers or customers in this way (most commonly from a fear of airing their dirty laundry in a semi-public setting), groups from within particular supplier or customer organisations can be used. Again, the purpose of the group setting is to find the most appropriate expression for their ideas, test how the different bits fit logically together, and assess how the ideas stack up against those held by their peers.

3. Summarising Documentary and Database Knowledge

In contrast to capturing the tacit knowledge held by staff (and customers and suppliers), capturing the explicit knowledge held in any organisation can be seen as a straightforward undertaking. The method used here is known as 'secondary source' analysis, and involves analysing those documents and records originally recorded for a different purpose. Needless to say, most organisations are awash in data – be they reports, databases, memos, policy documents, briefing papers, minutes from meetings or whatever. The key task is to ascertain whether any of those sources contain knowledge that could be applied in novel ways to improve the performance of the organisation.

What often prevents this analysis of secondary sources from being a straightforward undertaking in practice is that many organisations are poor at keeping track of what sources they have, at translating the information in those sources into a form that staff can meaningfully use, or even at feeding the information back to the level in the organisation at which the experience occurred. Moreover, some of our own experiences, and those of our colleagues, suggest that project outcomes are often repackaged to meet the expectations of clients. This may mean that the worst mistakes are ameliorated, reinterpreted as rare events, or attributed to previous systems or staff. In each case, the real opportunity to learn is lost.

The most common problem that confronts those embarking on secondary source analysis is knowing what sources exist, and how to find them. Sources that may prove to be a gold-mine to an organisation could be hidden away in a dusty corner of someone's office, or on a shelf where few people know of its existence ('shelfware', to use an expression we heard recently). This is why an important step in the identification phase involves having staff (at all levels in the organisation) brainstorm about the secondary sources they are aware of.

A second common problem is how to make sense of multiple sources. Most organisations have a great wealth of organisational memory tied up in secondary sources, but few have it in a form useful to most staff. For instance, it makes little sense to have a staff member trawl through a consultant's report looking for a single suggestion about how to work more effectively. A practical approach to provide a shorthand summary of relevant information is known as 'meta-knowledge' analysis. Meta-knowledge simply means knowledge about knowledge. The common meta-knowledge tools summarise existing knowledge sources and enable new interpretations (and conclusions) to be drawn from those sources. Meta-knowledge analysis involves the re-examination of existing data, such as research reports, board papers, memoranda, and so on, to draw new conclusions and make alternative interpretations relevant to a new set of research questions. Thus, the meta-knowledge process provides a summary of the organisation's existing secondary-source knowledge about a key issue.

4. Verifying the Utility of the Documentary and Database Knowledge, and Identifying the Gaps in the Collected Knowledge

Having summarised the key secondary sources available in your organisation, you are now in a position to assess the usefulness of those sources. One valuable way of doing this is to make use of 'gap analysis' techniques. As the name suggests, gap analysis uses the meta-knowledge summaries to highlight the gaps in the existing body of knowledge. It asks the question 'What is missing from what we already have?' Gap analysis highlights the gaps in the existing knowledge in terms of

- informational gaps (What topics of interest do we have no, or only insufficient, data about?);
- respondent gaps (Who haven't we heard from?); and

- credibility gaps (How much confidence can we have in the material in the meta-knowledge summary? How consistent are the findings, for instance? How do you reconcile competing perspectives? How can you know the data were collected in a rigorous way?).

A combined meta-knowledge and gap analysis provides organisations with a powerful technique to audit and target their knowledge gathering. Being clear about where the gaps in the existing knowledge are enables organisations to prioritise their future knowledge-gathering efforts. For instance: Can some of those gaps be filled from knowledge in books and articles? Are there courses that key staff can attend? Could one of your competitors (or suppliers) help? Do you need to do your own research? Is it time to get a consultant in? By being clear about what you need to know, and aware of what you already know, you are able to focus your future knowledge-gathering efforts. Interestingly, our experience is that these techniques can often save organisations money. We have completed a number of meta-knowledge analyses for clients in the past that made it clear the organisation didn't need to collect more information. What were desperately needed were mechanisms to get on top of the information that was already hidden throughout the organisation.

Step Two Outcomes

At the completion of step two (the reflection phase), you should be clear about

- what constitutes best practice (or best practices) for the various functional areas of your organisation (drawn from the knowledge held by your staff and recorded throughout the organisation in secondary source materials), and
- where the gaps in your existing knowledge are.

The products you should have completed are:

- a series of best practice (or best practices) descriptions, by functional areas;
- a collection of process improvement suggestions, by functional areas;
- a detailed index of existing secondary sources;
- a meta-knowledge summary of those secondary sources, by functional areas; and

○ a gap analysis, highlighting where future knowledge-gathering efforts need to be focused.

IDENTIFYING AND REFLECTING ON ORGANISATIONAL KNOWLEDGE: KEY QUESTIONS

Having completed the first two steps of the I-R-S-A process, an organisation should be able to answer the following four key questions:

What do we already know? How much of what you need to know is already known by your organisation? This may sound like a silly question, but it reinforces the idea that most organisations do not know what they already know. Is there someone in the organisation, or a report or paper somewhere, who knows something, or that contains something, that others need to know? Sources like past experiences and current expertise are the key to knowledge management. The challenges are getting access to that knowledge, finding ways to record it and make it accessible to others (and, ultimately, nurturing its future growth).

What do others already know? What do your suppliers, customers, and competitors (not to mention academics, consultants, etc.) know about your organisation that could be used to create competitive advantage?

Where are the gaps in our knowledge? Once you have audited the current level of relevant information in the organisation, it becomes a straightforward task to identify the gaps in your required knowledge. Identifying these gaps thus targets the future knowledge-gathering efforts of an organisation.

How do we fill those gaps? With the gaps identified, the next step is to choose the most appropriate ways to fill them. Where can you most productively target your future knowledge-gathering efforts? Where should you start?

Step Three: Share

The universe is made up of stories, not atoms.
- MURIEL RUCKEYSER

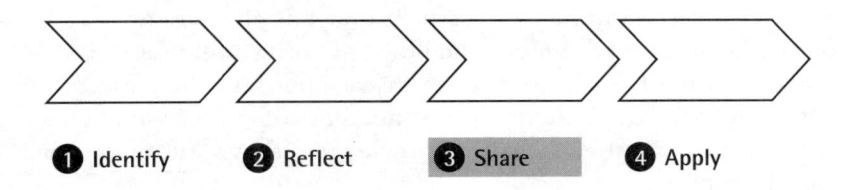

❶ Identify   ❷ Reflect   ❸ Share   ❹ Apply

Goal: To Make Knowledge that Exists Anywhere in Your Organisation Available Everywhere that It Is Needed

Once you have identified the key knowledge sources available in your organisation and assessed what you have to learn from those, the next step is to create effective mechanisms to make that knowledge available to the staff who need to know it. Consequently, once that knowledge has been identified and codified, the emphasis shifts to sharing it in the most effective ways possible.

The good news for any organisation embarking on a knowledge management project is that the I–R–S–A approach, by design, structures the sharing of knowledge into its processes (through group workshops and focus groups) or creates knowledge products that make knowledge sharing straightforward (meta-knowledge summaries, best practice checklists). This explains why the approach makes heavy use of group processes such as workshops and focus groups and attempts to limit the number of one-on-one methods. As well as being a forum for data gathering, and testing, the groups provide a powerful forum for teaching and learning. Our experience with such sessions is that participants inevitably learn new ways of doing things, or take away new ideas to contemplate. To ensure these processes do contribute to effective knowledge sharing, it is important that

- the group processes are facilitated in a way that requires the participation of all staff. Practical, hands-on, participatory exercises have proven most useful here. Furthermore, ensure the group sessions end with a definite debriefing round, where staff reflect on what they have learned from the session; and
- the meta-knowledge summaries are written in a way easily accessible to final users.

The key to achieving these outcomes is to have your own staff take part in the data collection activities. Although it is likely that most organisations will require outside help with group facilitation or focus group design, where possible in-house staff should be used. This not only maximises exposure and participation but also ensures that the knowledge uncovered through the process remains in-house.

Beyond the knowledge sharing that is built into the logic of the I–R–S–A approach, there are a number of easy-to-implement mechanisms that can help knowledge 'flow' through your organisation:

The Knowledge Map

We have already seen how creating a knowledge map provides a mechanism by which staff can access the knowledge they need to solve the problems they face everyday in their jobs. At a minimum, this map should include:

- a 'Yellow Pages' that lists where to find the resident experts throughout the organisation, and
- a list of frequently asked questions that distils out the important process lessons (see below).

In this regard, the knowledge map enables staff to 'pull' answers or suggestions from the knowledge management system rather than have them 'pushed' on to them. To ensure that people from different locations in the organisation know what others are talking about when they list their knowledge and knowledge sources, including a glossary and thesaurus with the knowledge map is an easy way to add value.

Frequently Asked Questions

The knowledge map should not only list the local experts for a particular issue or the secondary sources that relate to it but should also translate that expertise into an easy-to-follow guide to the stored knowledge. A good model is that provided by the frequently asked questions (FAQ) approach common to many Internet websites. Creating a list of FAQs involves having staff audit the key components of how they do their jobs. Two useful ways of thinking about this are in terms of (i) those components of the job that they would need to pass on to someone in order for that person to cover for them in their absence or (ii) the key lessons that need to be learned on induction to the job. The audit lists the frequently asked questions that would confront someone else doing their job, and then identifies where they need to go in the organisation to have those questions answered (both in terms of other staff and secondary sources). A simplified version of the FAQ list might look like that shown overleaf:

Frequently Asked Questions	Source of Solution:	
	Local Expertise	Secondary Sources
①		
②		
③		
④		
⑤		

Lessons Learned

Another useful addition to the knowledge map is a list of lessons learned from previous projects, jobs, customers, experiences, and so on. This might include checklists of what went right and what went wrong, leading to guidelines for similar future projects. This essentially creates a formal tool for capturing what was learned in the past so staff can do the job better and faster next time.

Tell Stories

We have talked about how storytelling (narrative) provides a powerful means of sharing tacit knowledge and capturing the lessons learned. John Seely Brown and Paul Duguid attribute much of this success to the fact that stories are good at presenting things sequentially (this happened, and then that happened) and good at identifying causes (this happened because of that). Moreover, the value of stories lies not just in their telling but also in their retelling. This means they provide a way that the 'old-timers' can pass on what they know to the newcomers (all Brown and Duguid, 2000:106-7). Where appropriate, stories should supplement the process lessons stored with the knowledge map. The 'learning history' approach of Art Kleiner and George Roth, from the MIT Center for Organizational Learning, provides one way that added meaning can be distilled from such stories.

LEARNING HISTORIES (KLEINER AND ROTH, 1998)

In the most basic terms, a 'learning history' is a written narrative of a company's recent set of critical episodes. These documents are written in two columns. In the right-hand column, the relevant events are described by those who took part in them, or were affected by them, or observed them close-up. The left-hand column contains analysis and commentary by the learning 'historians'. This is a small team of outsiders (usually consultants and academics) who identify the recurrent themes in the narrative, and pose questions about its assumptions and implications. The whole document is then used as the basis for group discussions about the lessons learned from the change episode. Check out www.solonline.org for more information.

Go Public
A simple and cheap way to create a knowledge-sharing exchange is to create a large 'knowledge sharing' board somewhere where staff cannot help seeing it (for instance, in the lunchroom or on the wall of a well-used hallway). The board can be used to list ideas, to elicit suggestions, and to inform staff about what is happening next.

Be Creative
How much knowledge do you think is lost to any organisation because it is buried in the middle of dense reports, or written in the language of memos or management rather than that of end users? Dean Acheson is purported to have said that 'a memorandum is written not to inform the reader but to protect the writer.' Equally, one of our friends has a sign above his desk that says 'a committee is a cul-de-sac down which ideas are lured and then quietly strangled.' The point being made in both cases is that the methods organisations have traditionally used to share information around their staff are remarkably ineffective. Even if there were nothing intrinsically wrong with the methods themselves, it would take a remarkable memo to cut through the clutter of all the memos that pile up on the desks of staff. Cutting through that clutter requires creativity. For instance, Ricardo Semler introduced the notion of the 'headline' memo in Semco. As he said: 'If you really want someone to evaluate a project's chances, only give them a single page to do it – and make them write a headline that gets to the point, as in a newspaper. There's no mistaking the conclusion of a memo that begins "New Toaster Will Sell 20,000 Units for $2 Million Profit"' (Semler, 1994:144).

Use Cross-Functional Exposure
One of the most effective ways to share knowledge throughout your organisation is to get staff who wouldn't normally talk to each other to start to do so. Many ideas grow better when transplanted into a

novel setting, and an excellent way to test your own assumptions about a particular problem is to talk to someone else who has a different set of assumptions about the problem's definition, components, and likely solution. As we will see in the next chapter, embedding systems that encourage staff to talk and listen to each other is the key to knowledge management. Initially, some simple steps that can be tried include:

- Install more water-coolers (or coffee machines, or Coke machines). The idea here is to create spaces where staff can bump into each other and talk informally about their work. As we've previously noted, although much office 'gossip' is not about work, a surprising amount of it is.
- Hold a knowledge fair. The term 'knowledge fair' may conjure up images of Ferris wheels and candy-floss, but it is used here to describe a structured opportunity for staff to meet and talk about their work. These can be serious 'trade show' kinds of affairs, or they can be as simple as a corporate picnic. Knowledge fairs are about creating opportunities for exchange between people who never get to meet during the course of their daily work. Remember, too, that less structure is always better for such fairs. Keeping a loose structure allows staff to 'pull' the knowledge they want from what is on show, rather than have it 'pushed' on to them according to whatever the organiser considers appropriate.

Appoint a Knowledge Manager

'Manager' here means someone with some influence in the organisation to act as a champion for the knowledge management project. Ultimately, knowledge management concerns what all the staff do all day. In this regard, successful knowledge management is about shifting the workplace culture. The knowledge manager therefore needs to play the roles of (i) an advocate of the project, (ii) a broker between knowledge holders, and (iii) an overseer of the content of the knowledge stocks and the systems used to make those stocks flow around the organisation. Consequently, the key skills required are those involved in making, leading, and sustaining relationships.

Create a Knowledge-Sharing Award

If organisations get what they reward, it makes sense to actively reward staff for knowledge-sharing behaviours. Ultimately, such behaviours should form part of the key performance indicators (KPIs) of all staff and contribute to promotion and rewards. However, in the immediate term, it is much easier to simply append a 'knowledge management award' onto the existing remuneration system. Different organisations will need to structure these in different ways to meet the needs of their own cultures. One model might be to have staff choose the insight they found most useful every month, and reward the person who provided it with a weekend away or dinner at a fine local restaurant. Create a prize that staff will want to strive for (like a weekend in a resort town) and make a big deal about the awards – thus creating the opportunity to use the awards to promote, and educate staff about, knowledge management.

Step Three Outcomes

At the completion of step three (the sharing phase), you should be clear about

- the knowledge that exists in your organisation, where it is, and how best to access that knowledge; and
- the most practicable methods for sharing that knowledge with the people in your organisation who most need to know it.

The products you should have completed are:

- a knowledge map, including: the 'Yellow Pages', FAQs, checklists, war stories, glossaries, and a thesaurus; and
- systems that match the organisation's existing culture and enable the most effective sharing of knowledge.

Step Four: Apply

What you know is not as important as what you do with it.
– DAVE ENGLISH

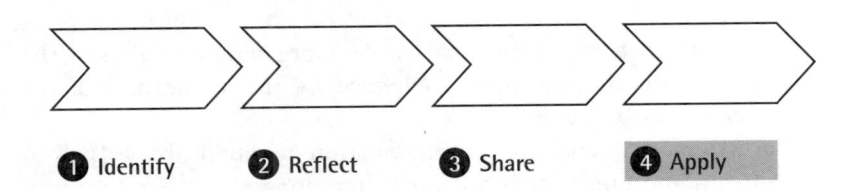

1 Identify **2** Reflect **3** Share **4** Apply

Goal: To Make the Best Use of the Knowledge Assets Available to You

The last phase of the I–R–S–A process is, in many regards, the most straightforward. It simply involves the application of knowledge assets to improve the way your organisation performs. As we have emphasised, knowledge management is all about 'knowledge in action'. The single reason organisations embark on a knowledge management strategy is to improve the way they perform (in the broadest possible sense).

The important point to make about 'application' is that there is a range of ways that staff can apply what they have learned. In many cases, what will change are the informal systems that staff use to get their jobs done. This means that, in the early days at least, the changes to the formal organisation will be minimal. One way to assist the application of new insights is to use part of the workshop sessions to ask staff 'How could we use this?' Where appropriate, action plans and time-frames could also be drawn up.

Over time, the application of knowledge should demonstrate tangible performance improvements. Where this occurs, the challenge is for organisations to go beyond merely applying such knowledge and create systems that embed that knowledge into their normal operating procedures. In this regard, the knowledge is transformed from human into structural capital. Where organisations take this challenge seriously, knowledge management provides an opportunity for the formal model of the organisation to move much closer to the informal reality of its day-to-day workings. In those instances where the application of knowledge does not demonstrate tangible performance improvements, the challenge is to audit the I–R–S–A process and discover why it seemed to promise to, and how processes can be changed to realise that promise.

Step Four Outcomes

At the completion of step four (the application phase), you should be clear about how to create the opportunities for staff to turn new knowledge into action.

The products you should have completed are:

○ a system that, over time, enables your organisation to assess the performance improvements delivered by the application of the new knowledge, and
○ a system that enables the organisation to audit the I–R–S–A process and fine-tune it for future iterations.

Managing the Risks

An important component of any new project is risk management. This involves identifying, analysing, evaluating, and treating the risks associated with the new project. So far, we have talked about applying the four-phase model as though this application is wholly unproblematic. In practice, there are a number of common risks associated with this kind of knowledge management project.

Failure to contribute

This is the risk that staff won't share their knowledge with others. In our experience, although this risk is very real, it hinges on how the project is set up and communicated. Demonstrating the intrinsic value of participation (thus answering the 'What's in it for me?' or 'WIIFM?'s at the outset) is the way to minimise this risk. Our view is that people are only too keen to share what they know with others when provided with a rationale and encouragement to do so. Trevor Williamson has this nice simile that the knowledge any one staff member has is like a library, only ever any use when the doors to the library are open. A closed library is of no use to anybody, and especially not the librarians.

Failure to Learn

This is the risk that staff won't listen to others. The corollary of the risk that staff won't contribute their knowledge (see above) is the risk that they won't draw from the knowledge of others. Again, in our experience, this risk is far more apparent than real and is contingent upon the way the project is sold to participants. Remember that much of the learning that occurs during the first two phases of the four-phase process is indirect, and thus sidesteps the overt resistance and cynicism of participants. The reality is that anyone who participates in the process cannot help but learn (bearing out Trevor's notion that 'you can't learn less').

Lack of Skills to Participate

There is a risk that staff will not have the necessary skills to communicate and articulate their knowledge, nor be able to actively engage with constructive criticism. The four-phase process is reliant on participants having the requisite maturity and social skills. Where these skills are not present, the process can break down.

Concerns over Confidentiality
Many organisations may be reluctant to approach their suppliers and customers to participate in a knowledge gathering (and sharing) project because (i) they are nervous about how the suppliers and customers will interpret this approach, or (ii) because they think this may risk sharing insights into the organisation that they would rather manage in confidence. Given that one of the goals of knowledge management is to create closer relationships with suppliers and customers (that is, increase customer and supplier capital), this reluctance has always struck us as being counterproductive.

Unrealistic Expectations
Because driving knowledge-sharing to the heart of the organisation does have the capacity to transform the organisation (see chapter seven), it is important that initial projects do not raise expectations among the staff of effecting change faster than the organisation can cope with or respond to. Unrealised expectations quickly become disinterest and cynicism. It is important, therefore, to make it clear to staff that organisational processes, structures, and cultures will all change, but none of them overnight. This means establishing the long-term vision for knowledge management and a series of interim milestones that can be worked towards.

Scope 'Creep'
There is so much knowledge available to any organisation that attempting to take control of it all will quickly seem overwhelming (and even quixotic). This means that even the smallest knowledge management project runs the risk of seeming like too much hard work. This is why we have emphasised the need to start small, remain focused, and develop a knowledge-management culture incrementally.

The above list outlines the risks associated with knowledge management at the project level. These are the risks we often see when dealing with organisations attempting to introduce the four-phase model outlined in this chapter. Although these risks are real (and, where handled poorly, can derail knowledge management at the outset), even greater risk is associated with the translation of knowledge management from a project to a process (that is, from the operational to the strategic level). The three most common risks here are identified below.

Failing to See the Strategic Value of Knowledge Management
This is the risk that organisations simply fail to translate the initial

project into a process embedded into the fabric of the workplace. We talked about this earlier in this chapter, under the heading 'Looking After the Goose That Lays the Golden Eggs'. Suffice it to say that – if knowledge sharing is to become the source of competitive advantage – knowledge management needs to become an integral part of organisational strategy.

Looking for 'Magic Bullets'

Not only are there no magic recipes for knowledge management, but there are no magic bullets, either. The risk some organisations face is that they will be looking for short cuts in all the wrong places. The two most obvious ones are putting too much faith in computers and putting too much faith in consultants. Knowledge management is about staff learning from other staff, and computers and consultants are only of any help to the extent that they facilitate and support that learning.

Lacking Focus

The most significant risk that organisations face is in pursuing knowledge that fails to address the real needs of the organisation. If knowledge sharing is to become the source of competitive advantage, then it is critical that organisations are clear about the kinds of knowledge that are required, when and where they are needed, and how that knowledge can be activated and applied.

The Value of Starting Small

This chapter has outlined an approach for getting started on knowledge management. It is a approach that begins with identifying the knowledge assets available to an organisation and ends with applying those assets in a way that improves some aspect of the organisation's performance. What this approach does particularly well is reflect a philosophy about how to manage knowledge. And, although the approach outlined here does contain a number of specific methodological tips, the model is premised on being sufficiently flexible so that organisations can adapt how they complete each of the I–R–S–A steps. This flexibility is a real strength of the approach but it also creates an important caveat: **the only way to discover which specific methods actually work in any organisational context is to try a range of them**, and this, in turn, means that it makes sense to start small. As we have just seen, this approach also offers a powerful way to manage the risks associated with introducing a knowledge management initiative into any organisation.

This caveat takes us back to the idea that has run throughout the chapters of this book — that there is no simple recipe for successful knowledge management. Individual organisations need to derive their own recipes from their own experiences. Logically, this means that organisations should start out along the path to knowledge management with a pilot scheme or case study. It makes little sense to adopt a widespread approach until the most appropriate methods have been identified. To do otherwise simply increases the chances of failure.

The key to creating an effective knowledge management strategy, then, is to start small. Not only will these modest efforts allow you to 'beta test' the methods that best suit your organisation but, ideally, they will also enable the success of those initial efforts to sell the value of knowledge management to staff. Once you find out what works for your organisation, you can then embed these techniques for future iterations of the I–R–S–A project cycle. The approach outlined in this chapter is necessarily project-like in focus. It is designed to get an organisation started on the road to knowledge management. The aim is that, over time, the overt knowledge-gathering mechanisms provided by the I–R–S–A cycle are replaced with organisational structures and processes which achieve the same goals, only as part of the everyday functioning of the organisation. The idea is to create an organisation that manages knowledge as a matter of course. The next chapter examines what that organisation might look like. In this regard, this chapter has provided the starting-point for a process of transition, with the kind of organisation outlined in the next chapter being the ultimate goal.

chapter seven

The Mature Knowledge-Managing Organisation

If we want things to stay as they are, things will have to change.
– GIUSEPPE DI LAMPEDUSA, *THE LEOPARD*.

Changing Places and Changing Rooms

In chapter five, we outlined what we see as the key elements of successful knowledge management; then, in chapter six, we talked about how to get started on a knowledge management project. In this chapter, we talk about what a mature knowledge-managing organisation might look like. This is the kind of organisation that has driven knowledge-sharing to the heart of the business, and one that has embedded the four essential functions we outlined in the last chapter (that is, the I–R–S–A approach) into its everyday operations.

We don't want to underplay the extent of the change required to achieve this kind of maturity, even though this chapter will be more concerned with the outcome than the process. Suffice it to say that, by now, it should be clear that any organisation serious about knowledge management will not be able to append a knowledge-centred culture onto an existing organisational form. 'Old-style business organizations don't manage knowledge well [precisely because] they weren't designed to' (Stewart, 1999:xxii). This book may have given the impression that transferring knowledge management best practice to conventional organisations is as easy as handing a colleague a doughnut in the tearoom. In reality, the transformation is 'more like an organ transplant, often rejected by the immune system' (Stamps, 1999).

While remaining conscious of the extent of change required, we also need to be clear that there are (obviously) many different possibilities for what a mature knowledge-managing organisation might actually look like. This is reflected in the vast literature on knowledge management, which includes best-practice examples as diverse as the US Army and Sun Microsystems. However, regardless of its actual form, we believe that any such organisation will incorporate many of the dimensions outlined here. For the sake of brevity, we have collapsed these dimensions into

- the knowledge organisation
- the knowledge manager
- the knowledge worker.

The Knowledge Organisation

Success in the knowledge economy 'depends on new skills and new kinds of organization and management'.
- THOMAS STEWART

This book has talked a great deal about how driving knowledge to the centre of your organisation will change that organisation in radical ways. We want to reiterate here that such a claim is not simply (more) consultant hyperbole. At the extreme end of the spectrum, driving knowledge to the centre of an organisation will transform the very nature of that organisation. Consider the example of a manufacturing company: focusing on the knowledge used to create the products could mean that the company ceases to manufacture anything at all, and moves to outsourcing production. In the process, the company shifts its core focus away from making things to product-design and marketing. In case this sounds implausibly far-fetched, consider that this is precisely what Nike – the most successful shoe manufacturer in the world – does. Out on the 'knowing edge', **knowledge replaces production**.

Slightly less radical is the notion that **knowledge replaces premises**. In chapter one, we talked about how 'weightlessness' was a characteristic of the products and services of the companies out on that knowing edge. This means that many companies do not need large premises to make or store their products. Twice in the process of writing this book we were reminded of this fact: the first time was while purchasing a small piece of software we needed and the second was when chasing down a report we wanted to cite. In both cases, we simply went to the appropriate web page, gave out our credit card details, and downloaded the relevant exe file or pdf document. No need to store, wrap, ship, and bill for either product. And 'delivery' was instantaneous. Buying and selling never used to be like this. Yet it is a trend that is increasingly obvious in retailing. In the USA, for instance, Hallmark has introduced kiosks where customers can have a personalised greeting card printed while they wait. We have all seen those business card machines that do the same at airports. In New Zealand, much of the debate around the recent Warner-EMI merger was about how customers will soon be able to download the music they want directly from the World Wide Web, thus cutting out the retailer altogether. The same applies to online shopping houses such as Amazon.com and all the other e-tailers – organisations that have no shops in the traditional sense of the word. Instead, in one regard, their shops exist anywhere anyone has access to the Internet and a credit card. Finally, even the most conservative banks now offer Internet banking services 'open' for 24 hours a day, and there is a whole new breed of banks – such as Bank Direct – that have no conventional premises at all.

Even for organisations that continue to make and sell things in a conventional way, focusing on knowledge will alter how those conventional processes are supported. For instance, to take an obvious example, **knowledge replaces inventory**. One of knowledge's most powerful advantages is 'its ability to wipe out inventory' (Stewart, 1999:24). In the past, inventory was more important than information because information could never be precise enough to control inventory. Consequently, companies covered up for this imprecision by keeping more stock on hand, 'just in case' it was needed. The rise of just-in-time (JIT) manufacturing is really about the triumph of JIT inventory control. The 'kanban' (index card) replaces the warehouse. In the words of Thomas Stewart:

> There's a simple but powerful lesson to be drawn here: every bin of parts, every pallet of raw material, every uncollected bill, every piece of paper in transit from one person's in-box to another ties up time and money to no useful purpose ... and driving it out is one of the first ways in which investments in information and knowledge can boost corporate performance (Stewart, 1999:29).

So much for the radical possibilities of 'mature' knowledge managing. Let's now have a closer look at some of the key elements likely to be present in any organisation that takes knowledge-sharing seriously.

Organisational Structures and Processes

Peter Drucker (1998) writes about 'three periods' of organisational change in the Western industrialised countries. The first period, covering 1895 to 1905, refers to how management became distinct from ownership. The second period, from the mid 1920s until the mid 1950s, deals with how the 'command and control' hierarchy became the dominant mode of industrial organisation throughout the world (with its reliance upon departments and divisions). The third period, which we are currently experiencing, deals with the shift to 'the information-based organization, the organization of knowledge specialists' (1998:19). Drucker's three-period taxonomy reinforces what we have argued for throughout this book: that, in knowledge-centred organisations, getting the most out of human, structural, and customer/supplier capital demands a new kind of organisational *culture* (see below). Unfortunately, for those organisations serious about knowledge, you cannot simply mandate a new culture. Organisational culture is at best a secondary phenomenon (and, perhaps even more accurately, an epiphenomenon). What organisations can do is change the *structures* and *strictures* which help shape culture (such as management styles, reward structures, hiring policies, training regimes, etc.). These both signal the new culture and provide a catalyst for its realisation. We think the key elements of structure in the mature knowledge-managing organisation include:

Human Resources

Given that knowledge management is all about organisational learning, and that the only parts of any organisation that ever truly 'learn' are its staff, it is no surprise that how it deals with its staff is a key dimension of the mature knowledge-managing organisation.

- **Staffing:** mature knowledge-managing organisations have active policies to ensure: that they recruit staff rich in human capital; that those recruits are thoroughly enculturated into the organisation; that they are constantly challenged (and are learning on a continuous basis); that they are rewarded commensurate with the value they add to the organisation; and that there are mechanisms in place to ensure smooth succession of staff (in case of promotion within the organisation or staff leaving for elsewhere).
- **Recruitment:** recognising the value of informal learning, mature knowledge-managing organisations use recruitment procedures: that value curiosity and experience as much as formal qualifications; that match learning and working preferences with the dominant organisational culture; that involve staff who will be working with the recruit in the selection process; and that look to nurture talent from within the organisation before outsourcing.

- **Induction:** 'induction' into a mature knowledge-managing organisation is an intricate process better conceptualised as a structured (and ongoing) process of 'enculturation'. This involves processes such as: assigning all new recruits with a mentor and a 'buddy'; using peer review to assess their integration; and matching induction tasks to the level of skill, maturity, and learning style of the recruit. (Where appropriate, the mature knowledge-managing organisation is not averse to throwing new talent in at the deep end.)
- **Training:** the mature knowledge-managing organisation invests heavily in training for its staff. This training is related to the organisation's broader goals and the staff's personal goals through the use of competency maps. These maps ensure this learning is matched to the learning styles of the staff. In some cases, the mature knowledge-managing organisation devolves the responsibility for training to its staff by providing (generous) resources to support training opportunities while leaving them to find the best way to fulfil their needs. Achievement of learning goals is an important criterion used in performance reviews. Finally, the mature knowledge-managing organisation recognises that the formal training is only a subset of the learning that occurs in the workplace (see below).
- **Rewards and promotion:** as James Fallows (1997) tells us: 'any organization works best when the behavior that helps an individual get ahead is also the behavior that benefits the organization as a whole.' Obviously, the mature knowledge-managing organisation rewards staff for creating and sharing knowledge. The size of these rewards is commensurate with the value which that knowledge adds to the organisation (and often involves a measure of organisational equity). Promotions are based on knowledge contributions, and staff are encouraged to be both innovative and critical (mistakes are not penalised). Promotions are closely tied to peer reviews of performance and contribution. In general, the kinds of rewards provided are tailored to the needs of individual staff (for example, different people at different stages of the life cycle may choose more time off or more flexibility over more money).
- **Performance management:** we noted above that the mature knowledge-managing organisation makes intensive use of peer reviews to assess the performance of staff. The culture of the workplace is also one that strives to constantly 'raise the stakes' on knowledge workers. Mature knowledge-managing organisations

have a high-performance culture that keeps their staff challenged (through providing more tasks, different kinds of tasks, or novel tasks). However, these organisations also have the support systems in place to assist staff reach these new goals (reviews, training, mentoring, buddying, etc.).
- **Succession planning:** by constantly challenging staff, mature knowledge-managing organisations recognise that they also need to regularly provide staff with new opportunities. Consequently, mature knowledge-managing organisations have career plans in place for their staff. These plans may involve movement within the organisation but can also involve moving outside the organisation. These organisations recognise that some of their talented workers are always going to leave them for larger challenges and assist the staff to upskill to meet the positions they desire. Why mature knowledge-managing organisations do this, in part, is because it provides a powerful mechanism with which to map and plan for staff succession (and to ensure the continuity of knowledge). Staff members in line for promotions, or new positions outside the organisation, thus understand their commitment to mentor their replacements before they move.

KNOWLEDGE MANAGEMENT AND HAPPY STAFF

Katherine Corich, the founder of the New Zealand knowledge management company Sysdoc, has been described by *Unlimited* magazine as 'a boss to die for', and her company touted as 'a Kiwi firm that really does do human resources with imagination' (Mandow, 2001). Looking at the success of Sysdoc, *Unlimited* magazine identified eight simple principles to ensure a happy staff:

- Employ people with similar professional and ethical values.
- Create salary and incentive packages around an individual's motivations, not what's easiest for the company.
- Offer flexible work options.
- Ensure good communication mechanisms so staff feel part of the team.
- Build teams where individuals support and nurture one another to achieve professional goals.
- Ensure employees' career aspirations are regularly reviewed and a career path is established.
- Be prepared to think 'outside the square' when dealing with staff issues.
- 'Set people free' – encourage people who are making positive changes in their lives.

Workplace Learning

As well as a commitment to staff training, the mature knowledge-managing organisation recognises the wealth of learning that occurs throughout the workplace and has systems in place to maximise those opportunities.

- **Structured learning opportunities:** mature knowledge-managing organisations structure processes such as 'after action reviews' (AARs) into every project cycle (or, for those organisations that do not work on a project basis, as part of a regular team review). These processes embed reflection and the systematic recording of lessons learned (mistakes made, ideas for the future, etc.) into the fabric of work. In some mature knowledge-managing organisations there are dedicated 'learning historians' who work alongside project teams to continuously record the lessons learned during any project cycle.
- **Cross-functional exposure:** mature knowledge-managing organisations make intensive use of cross-functional project teams. These include participants from a vertical and horizontal slice through the organisation. In order to ensure these teams function effectively, there are clear guidelines and dispute resolution processes in place. Beyond specific project teams, there are regular meetings where staff from different parts of the organisation learn about one another's problems. 'Creative abrasion' is actively pursued as an integral part of the workplace culture.
- **Forums where staff can share ideas with one another:** beyond involvement in cross-functional project teams and meetings, mature knowledge-managing organisations also ensure there are plenty of informal spaces where staff from throughout the organisation can talk to one another. For some, this means lots of water-cooler spaces, coffee pots, and Coke machines. For others, it is plush 'chill-out' spaces. These are supplemented with regular knowledge fairs and other kinds of events which maximise the exposure of staff to each other.
- **Communities of practice:** communities of practice are recognised as a key resource to mature knowledge-managing organisations. This means these organisations resource these communities and provide whatever support the members of the communities need.

○ **Time and space to share knowledge:** finally, mature knowledge-managing organisations recognise that the key to successful knowledge sharing (and creation) is providing staff with the time they need to do 'knowledge work'. This means that knowledge work is seen as a legitimate part of the working day, and that staff are encouraged to dedicate a portion of their working day to it (for example, by having a time-sheet code for knowledge work, or by ensuring the working day is sufficiently porous that staff are able to think, reflect, and talk). Mature knowledge-managing organisations recognise that the amount of 'slack' time provided to staff for learning and thinking is one of the best metrics for a firm's commitment to becoming a knowledge-centred organisation (Davenport and Prusak, 1998:93). As well as time, mature knowledge-managing organisations also provide dedicated spaces for staff to do knowledge work (for example, 'break out' rooms and offices). In other organisations, 'creating space' is reflected in a changed office layout.

Computing Systems

In mature knowledge-managing organisations, the computer systems are designed to support the creation and sharing of knowledge. This means that they incorporate

○ **a knowledge directory:** the computer system provides an easy-to-use, single point of entry into the knowledge databases. This is a 'stepped entry system' where staff enter their question or area of interest and are provided with a FAQ list; if this fails to answer their need, the directory then takes staff to more detailed documentary resources as well as highlighting who in the organisation is the resident expert in that area. This kind of system means staff are able to 'pull' the information they want from it; it is easy to use; and it becomes the first point of reference for any problem or question.

○ **a knowledge network:** the computer system captures 'living' knowledge by being continuously updated by users. This means that anyone can add new content, or provide a commentary on the ideas offered by others. To ensure this is done effectively, staff are trained to (i) recognise important learning moments (through reflection) and (ii) write succinctly and clearly about those moments. The system is administered by a database manager, who

THE MATURE KNOWLEDGE-MANAGING ORGANISATION

acts as a moderator for any ongoing debates and plays the crucial role of purging content from the system (both by moving things to a separate archive and by liberal use of the 'delete' function).
- **evolution:** to ensure the computer system continues to meet the needs of staff, mature knowledge-managing organisations have computer systems that evolve organically. This evolution is driven by a project team that is heavily loaded with users rather than systems or computer experts.

Performance Management

In mature knowledge-managing organisations, the contribution of knowledge sharing to the 'bottom line' is clearly understood. This means that the organisation can identify high-value knowledge projects, and pursue the kinds of innovations that continue to deliver competitive advantage. These organisations do this through:

- **strategic planning:** knowledge is understood to be a strategic resource, and systems are in place to ensure the organisation can forecast its future knowledge needs (albeit with a healthy measure of respect for the uncertainty which comes with being in knowledge markets). Given this uncertainty, flexibility is highly valued.
- **business development:** although knowledge creation and sharing is driven to the heart of the business, this does not mean that mature knowledge-managing organisations do not also have specific functions dedicated to knowledge creation. A proportion of revenue is dedicated to R&D and education. There are R&D departments that resemble 'skunk works'. Staff are seconded from the organisation to work in this department, and the scientists and researchers running the department are cycled through sabbaticals outside of the lab and on the shop-floor.
- **external benchmarking:** one way that mature knowledge-managing organisations measure their performance is by benchmarking against competitors. They rely heavily on systems that expose the organisation (and the teams within it) to external perspectives and practices. As well as benchmarking performance measures, mature knowledge-managing organisations also have formal and informal forums in place where people from outside the organisation can come to share their practices and tips.
- **holistic performance measures:** we like to think that mature knowledge-managing organisations see their success in terms

broader than simply revenues and profits. In our ideal mature knowledge-managing organisation, performance is measured according to something like the triple bottom line, where the organisation measures itself according to its financial, environmental, and social wealth.

Workplace Management

This section should have made it clear that mature knowledge-managing organisations require a different approach to management from that of conventional organisations. We particularly like Peter Drucker's idea that mature knowledge-managing organisations 'will resemble symphony orchestras more than large factories' (see below). This will be evident through:

○ **input into decision making:** becoming 'knowledge-centred' means mature knowledge-managing organisations devolve decision making to those best placed in the organisation to make the decisions (that is, they put into practice 'decephalisation'). This is what Chan Kim and Renée Mauborgne label 'engagement', noting it 'communicates management's respect for individuals and their ideas, [it] sharpens everyone's thinking and builds better collective wisdom. Engagement results in better decisions by management and greater commitment from all involved in executing those decisions' (1997:69). The goal here is to create a workplace where staff feel as though they are autonomous and responsible, true partners in the business.

○ **new roles for management:** in mature knowledge-managing organisations, managers understand that their role is to create the right environment for knowledge workers to get on with their jobs. Instead of the old focus on managers planning, organising, executing, and measuring (POEM), managers in the mature knowledge-managing organisations see their job as one of defining, nurturing, and allocating (DNA). Beyond this, mature knowledge-managing organisations have a senior manager dedicated to ensuring the development of knowledge stocks and flows. This chief knowledge officer (CKO) is a member of the organisation's senior management team and, reflecting the recognition of the value knowledge contributes to the organisation, is as prized as the chief financial officer (CFO).

Organisational Culture

The purpose of the structural and process changes outlined above is to create an organisation where staff identify, reflect upon, share, and apply knowledge as part of their daily routines. All this takes place within the context of an organisation that is clear about the contribution knowledge makes to its competitive advantage and the steps necessary to nurture and reproduce that knowledge.

Clearly, this is a culture high in trust, where knowledge sharing is the norm, and these knowledge-sharing behaviours are modelled from the very top of the organisation. As with the Hewlett Packard example in chapter five, all the knowledge in the organisation is available to all staff unless expressly forbidden (that is, the onus is always on managers to justify restrictions they place on access to information). Equally, this is a culture that is decidedly 'open', where constructive criticism is expected and even welcomed; one where pointing out the potential flaws in the ideas of a colleague or a superior is seen as a positive contribution rather than an act of insubordination. This flows from an understanding that everyone in the organisation is knowledgeable and, potentially, has a contribution to make. What matters is the quality of the ideas and not their origin.

It is hard to overstate what a radical departure this kind of culture would be from conventional organisations. We like the example of Sun Microsystems in the early days of the World Wide Web's development. As Robert Austin describes it:

> If we are to give Sun's managers credit ... it is not for their ability to clearly see the future. Rather, it is because they tolerated and even nurtured the 'out-of-controlness' that sometimes distresses us as managers ... Sun has a culture in which the techies push back when managers do something dumb. In such a culture, change can come from anywhere in the company. But it's not always pretty – or orderly (2001:50).

This is the kind of workplace where staff think it is perfectly natural to ask others in the organisation, even senior staff, for the help they need. It is also one where talking to others, reading at work, or even sitting quietly and thinking are seen as legitimate work. Finally, this is the kind of workplace where staff feel a sense of ownership and are excited to be. This is reflected in high rates of staff retention and low rates of absenteeism.

We know that, laid out like this, the mature knowledge-managing organisation seems somewhat like a Utopian manifesto. But we need to reiterate that such organisations are first and foremost about the creation of sustainable competitive advantage. We often say that the structure and culture outlined here offer an ideal that organisations can only ever approximate. However, we are also aware that the environment at Sun Microsystems sounds far from ideal to many people. Yet this apparent 'out-of-controlness' is driven by the logic of innovation and learning. Moreover, many of the structural changes outlined above lead to a virtuous cycle. To use that most over-used of words, these structural changes create 'synergies'. Or as Paulo Freire put it: 'once you start a person thinking there is no telling where they will go …'

In case you think our notion of the mature knowledge-managing organisation is too radical, we thought you would like to know how some other commentators see such organisations developing. Here is the vision according to the 'big three' of Peter Drucker, Ikujiro Nonaka, and David Garvin:

PETER DRUCKER'S INFORMATION-BASED ORGANISATIONS

Drucker (1998) argues that businesses 20 years from now will resemble symphony orchestras more than large factories. They will have a 'score' (a set of clear, simple objectives that translate into particular actions) and a structure where everyone takes responsibility for their own information needs. This means employees will need to specialise, and any organisation of specialists is stifled by traditional command and control structures. Moreover, these specialists will be found throughout the operational side of the business and not in the old head office. 'In the information-based organization, the knowledge will be primarily at the bottom' (1998:6). Consequently, the number of management levels and the numbers of managers can be sharply reduced. 'The best example of a large and successful information-based organization has no middle management at all' (1998:7). The key to such organisations it to have everyone asking 'Who depends on me for what information?' and 'On whom do I depend for information?' This includes superiors and subordinates but should mostly involve colleagues. 'Everyone in an organisation should constantly be thinking through what information he or she needs to do the job and make a contribution' (1998:11). Reward structures have to change to support the new organisation, and promotion will be within a speciality rather than the company. Drucker is clear – 'whatever scheme is eventually developed will work only if the values and compensation structure of business are drastically changed' (1998:14). The key challenge in this organisation of specialists is how to meld a common vision. Drucker's solution is to use 'task forces' for this purpose. 'The information-based business will use more and more smaller self-governing units' (Drucker, 1998:25). However, although this solves the problem of coordination it also raises one of management: who will manage the enterprise? If it is those that lead the task forces, then what happens when a given task is complete? Also, how will you choose the company's top management without the levels of middle management working as proving grounds for management skills? The answer is provided by the German Gruppe where the decentralised units are set up as separate companies with their own top managements (and the Germans use this model precisely because of their tradition of promoting people in their specialities – especially in research and engineering).

IKUJIRO NONAKA'S 'KNOWLEDGE-CREATING COMPANY'

Nonaka (1998) is clear that knowledge offers the only source of 'lasting competitive advantage' in the new economy. However, few companies optimise the rewards of that knowledge because they misunderstand what it is and what they need to do to leverage it. Traditional organisations see the only useful knowledge as that which is formalised and systematic. In contrast, major Japanese companies such as Honda, Canon, Matsushita, NEC, and Sharp have built their reputations by having an entirely different approach to managing the creation of new knowledge. 'The centrepiece of this approach is the recognition that creating new knowledge is not simply a matter of "processing" objective information [but] it depends on tapping the tacit and often highly subjective insights, intuitions, and hunches of individual employees ...' (1998:24). This 'more holistic approach to knowledge is also founded on another fundamental insight: a company is not a machine but a living organism' (1998:25). Thus, the organisation has a collective sense of identity and a fundamental purpose. 'This is the organizational equivalent of self-knowledge' (1998:25). 'In the knowledge-creating company, inventing new knowledge is not a specialized activity – the province of the R&D department or marketing or strategic planning. It is a way of behaving, indeed a way of being, in which everyone is a knowledge worker' (1998:25). Knowledge creation needs to be at the centre of an organisation's human resources strategy. The knowledge-creating company is all about creating the structures, and the culture, so that personal knowledge is available to others. This needs to take place at all levels and functions of the organisation, and to take place continuously. It is about taking the tacit knowledge of staff and turning it into useful explicit knowledge (where, ideally, one person's tacit knowledge is turned into explicit knowledge that, by becoming integrated into the operations of the organisation, becomes everyone's tacit knowledge). The process of converting tacit knowledge into explicit knowledge Nonaka labels 'articulation'. The process of turning that knowledge back into widespread tacit knowledge he calls 'internalization'. Together they delineate the spiral of knowledge that is critical in a knowledge-creating company (1998:30). The key is how to articulate that tacit knowledge. Nonaka talks about the role that speaking figuratively and using metaphors plays. These provide means by which people can 'put together what they know in new ways and begin to express what they know but cannot yet say' (Nonaka, 1998:34).

DAVID GARVIN'S LEARNING ORGANISATION

Garvin (1998) defines a 'learning organisation' as one that is 'skilled at creating, acquiring, and transferring knowledge, and at modifying its behavior to reflect new knowledge and insights' (1998:51). This definition highlights the fact that, to count as a 'learning organisation', it is not enough to generate new knowledge: organisations also need to act on that knowledge. Continuous improvement involves a commitment to learning. Learning organisations are thus skilled at five main activities (1998:52-3):

- systematic problem-solving
- experimentation with new approaches
- learning from their own experience and history
- learning from the experiences and best practices of others, and
- transferring knowledge quickly and efficiently through the organisation.

It is by creating systems and processes that support these five activities, and by integrating them into the fabric of daily operations, that companies begin to manage their learning more effectively. Garvin is clear that learning organisations are 'not built overnight' but can be approximated by the creation of structures which

- foster an environment that is conducive to learning;
- give employees the time and space to reflect and analyse;
- train employees in common methods of problem-solving;
- open up boundaries within the organisation and encourage/stimulate the exchange of ideas (cross-function meetings, presentations, seminars, etc.); and
- create learning forums. 'These are programs or events designed with explicit learning goals in mind' (1998:76).

Finally, you can see what 'real' mature knowledge-managing organisations look like by checking out the winners of the annual 'Most Admired Knowledge Enterprises' (MAKE) award, and the members of the 'MAKE Hall of Fame' at www.knowledgebusiness.com.

The Knowledge Manager

My definition of a free society is a society where it is safe to be unpopular.
- ADLAI STEVENSON

As will be clear by now, driving knowledge-sharing to the centre of the business will change everything for managers. First, we have seen how

Peter Drucker foresees organisations where 'the number of management levels and the numbers of managers can be sharply reduced', and 'the best example of a large and successful information-based organization has no middle management at all' (1998:7). A less radical interpretation (or even an interim one) is that the nature of the management role itself will change. Ricardo Semler notes that:

> ... when we started sharing information at Semco it had such a profound effect. People in the higher echelons could no longer rely on the conventional symbols and had to develop leadership skills and knowledge to inspire respect. The centres of power shifted (1994:277).

There is a good argument that the one job that will change beyond all recognition in the knowledge economy is that of management. As we all know, traditional management is a legacy of Frederick Winslow Taylor's brilliant insight into the nature of 'time and motion'. Under this regime, workers were given specific tasks to do, a set time to do it in, and any number of supervisors and managers were employed to ensure they did it exactly so. For the worker, this meant 'drudgery, constant repetition, and narrow job descriptions' (Stewart, 1999:48), but, for the industrial economy as a whole, the system was a master-stroke.

In contrast to industrial production, with its 'manager knows best' approach to knowledge, the knowledge economy is built on entirely different ways of working. It has a professional flavour precisely because, as we have noted several times throughout this book, everything comes to resemble a professional service ('congealed knowledge' rather than 'congealed resources'). And this means that a new approach to management is required:

> The explosion of scientific and technical knowledge, the rapid diffusion and fast-growing power of information technology, knowledge's increasing share of corporate value-added, the rise of the knowledge worker — all of these work together ... to force new kinds of organizational design and new managerial method and substance (Stewart, 1999:49).

Think of it in these terms: knowledge workers are able to plan, organise, and execute their own work. This means that there is no need for managers to be preoccupied with telling people what to do or how to do it. Instead, what knowledge workers need is someone to lead them and to marshal the resources they need to support them. So management becomes about setting the vision and the goals the company can work towards, and ensuring the workforce have the resources they need to carry out their jobs effectively.

Not only does the *purpose* of management shift in the knowledge economy, so does its *nature*. With the rise of networked organisations, there will be a corresponding decline in the power of hierarchies. In practice:

- networks *enable different kinds* of interaction. For instance: they overcome distance by enabling staff to work removed from each other; they overcome traditional organisational boundaries by enabling staff to work together regardless of their department; and
- networks *encourage different styles* of interaction. For instance: e-mail is more direct, less deferential, and more informal than conventional alternatives.

It is for reasons like these that networks are incompatible with old-style 'command and control' hierarchies. To quote Chan Kim and Renée Mauborgne again:

> **Creating and sharing knowledge are activities that can neither be supervised nor forced out of people. They happen only when people co-operate willingly ... getting that active co-operation may well turn out to be one of the key managerial issues of the next few decades (1997:71).**

The new challenge for managers is to provide the right environment to allow the knowledge workers to get on with their jobs. As noted in the section on workplace structures and processes, this means that the focus of management moves away from the old POEM (plan, organise, execute, measure) to a new DNA (define, nurture, allocate) (Stewart, 1999:191). This means managers need to

- **define** what needs to be done, keep the projects focused on that goal (What are you doing, for whom?), and link the project to the direction the organisation is heading in. Managers will constantly reassess issues like 'What business are we in?' and 'What value do we seek to offer our customers?'
- **nurture** the intellectual assets (human, structural, and customer/supplier) needed to achieve the goals and ends defined.

This involves answering questions like 'What knowledge assets are essential to our business?' 'How do we get them?' and 'How do we keep them at their best?' The 'nurture' focus extends to customers and suppliers, and deals with questions like 'How can we develop closer relationships with our customers and suppliers?'.
○ **allocate** resources to the opportunities identified. Through the allocation of resources, management makes choices about which projects will be privileged over others. This involves answering questions like 'Which of these projects is the best one for the business right now?', 'What do we need to make it work?', and 'What's the best way to get those resources?'

As we have already intimated, the changing emphasis will please some managers but will be exasperating to others. The managers at Sun Microsystems may have engaged well with the new demands on them but many others will simply see it as a challenge to their traditional sources of authority and prestige. Stephen Denning puts it like this:

> Everyone is to a greater or lesser extent aware that the [shift to knowledge-centred organisations] entails a shift from an organization that has operated vertically and hierarchically to one that will operate horizontally and collaboratively across organizational borders. For some this means deliverance. But those whose careers have flourished in mastering the vertical hierarchical pathways have different attitudes towards the shift (2001:27).

Those with different attitudes towards the shift can also prove a significant 'site of resistance' to the pursuit of becoming knowledge-centred.

In 1988, Shoshana Zuboff wrote *In the Age of the Smart Machine: The Future of Work and Power*. This book, very popular and influential in its day, argued that computers had the ability to change the nature of management because they could distribute management information to the workforce. By opening access to what was once management knowledge, the technology could change forever the role of the manager. This is relevant here because many of the claims made for knowledge management echo those articulated by Zuboff over a decade ago. What is particularly pertinent is why Zuboff believes the potential of computers was never realised. She tells us:

> The paradise of shared knowledge and a more egalitarian working environment just isn't happening ... knowledge isn't shared because management doesn't want to share authority and power (quoted in Brown and Duguid, 2000:30).

Chan Kim and Renée Mauborgne make the same point when they write that some managers:

> retain power only by keeping what they know to themselves. Their implicit strategy is to preserve their managerial discretion by deliberately leaving the rules for success and failure vague. Other managers maintain control by keeping employees at arm's length, substituting memos and forms for direct, two-way communication, thus avoiding the challenges to their ideas and authority (1997:74).

The simple lesson here is that managers are critical to the success of creating a knowledge-centred organisation. And although there are exciting new challenges awaiting managers in that kind of organisation, many managers would just as soon wait. It is important, therefore, to create mechanisms that enrol managers in the change process from the outset.

Enter the Chief Knowledge Officer

No discussion about the changing role of management would be complete without a brief mention of the importance of the chief knowledge officer (CKO) to any knowledge-centred organisation. We have already talked about how the CKO is a new position, dedicated to ensuring the development of knowledge stocks and flows, and about how such a position is as prized as the CFO. The core responsibility of the CKO can be seen as facilitating organisational learning, which means that CKOs need to

- advocate knowledge and learning,
- lead the development of the knowledge-management strategy,
- design and implement a knowledge infrastructure,
- create the means and climate for knowledge creation and communication throughout the organisation,
- manage relationships with outside knowledge and information providers, and
- measure and manage the value of knowledge.

The one danger with creating the position of CKO (and especially for those organisations that do it too soon into the change process) is that it can signal to staff that the CKO will take *responsibility* for the creation and sharing of knowledge rather than simply *lead the organisation* to that creation and sharing. The idea is not to create a new organisational silo responsible for knowledge management (in its broadest sense) but to enable staff everywhere in the organisation to manage knowledge. As Davenport and Prusak tell us, 'the most successful knowledge organisations are those where knowledge management is part of everyone's job' (1998:107).

The Knowledge Worker

You can't think rationally on an empty stomach, and a whole lot of people can't do it on a full one either.
- LORD REITH

If becoming knowledge-centred will change the very nature of the organisation, and transform the role and style of management beyond recognition, then what will it do for the 'typical' worker? In many ways, this discussion takes us back to the very first chapter of the book, where we talked about the broader changes occurring in the 'new' economy. To put that another, more enigmatic, way: the nature of work will change because the nature of work has changed.

The new economy has already created an entirely new class of worker whose jobs revolve around manipulating knowledge. These are what sociologists call the 'symbolic analysts' and, significantly, include all the best jobs in the new economy: the lawyers, consultants, engineers, designers, advertising executives, professors, and so on. Indeed, anybody who performs 'problem solving, problem identifying, and strategic-brokering activities' (Reich, 1992:177).

What is interesting, sociologically, is that these jobs are service sector jobs. Interesting because the growth of the service sector used to be seen (and in some circles still is seen) negatively, as though solid primary and secondary sector jobs would be replaced by people flipping burgers at Burger King or cleaning toilets at Holiday Inn. In reality, the growth of the service sector has been about 'an explosion of well-paid knowledge worker jobs' (Stewart, 1999:41). Indeed, there is almost a direct link between the extent of problem-solving, problem-identifying, and strategic-brokering activities involved in a job and its level of rewards.

Perhaps even more significant than the rise of the symbolic analysts is the fact that *all jobs now involve more knowledge work than they once did*. In other words, all workers will become knowledge workers to a greater or lesser extent. Think of examples like farming (where software is used to plan crop harvests and rotations); car assembly (where TQM and JIT systems demand numeracy skills as a minimum); car mechanics (where sophisticated diagnostic equipment is common); and office work (with its reliance on IT). Even the army, once the refuge of the truly unemployable, requires an ability to deal with serious amounts of information. Technology certainly removes some kinds of jobs but it also creates new jobs by transforming work. And, because of the changing composition of these jobs, manufacturers are employing better educated workers. The good news for 'typical' workers is that becoming better educated means being able to command a higher premium for their skills. In the words of Thomas Stewart (1999:44), 'labour markets reward people who work with their brains and slap around those who do not' (see note 10, page 174).

Careers With Mature Knowledge-Managing Organisations

The changing nature of work means career paths are not what they used to be. Thomas Stewart suggests seven ways that careers will necessarily change for 'typical' workers (Stewart, 1999:206-217):

- A career becomes a series of 'gigs' rather than a series of steps. Careers no longer progress 'up' 'ladders' but by the richness of the work and the size of the contribution made. 'What distinguishes a star ... is not his (sic) level in the organization but the complexity and value of the projects he works on' (Stewart, 1999:206). The résumé of the future will show few changes of job title but many changes of employer.
- Project management becomes the key to successful careers. Whereas once upon a time special projects were the province of the moribund within the corporation, now they are the centre of strategy. As routine work becomes increasingly self-managing, it is the new projects that will create new value.
- Power will flow from expertise, not position. In the flat structures that characterise mature knowledge-managing organisations, authority comes from knowing. Those who are seen as authoritative are those who create the most value for the organisation. Experience will count here as much as expertise.
- You will not have to work *for* the organisation to work *with* it. The number of freelance professionals ('independent resource providers')

will continue to increase as organisations increasingly identify where their existing knowledge assets can add the most value.
- Careers will be in markets, not hierarchies. Even for employees, thinking like the self-employed is the best way to manage a career. (Think: 'Who is my competition?', 'What do I offer that keeps me ahead of them?' and 'Where is the market (inside the organisation as well as outside) for my skills?')
- The fundamental career choice becomes between specialising and generalising. Careers will be defined less by companies ('I work for Boeing') than by professional specialities ('I design control systems'). In the words of one commentator, 'loyalty has been replaced by integrity' (Parker, 2000:D1).
- Intellectual capital will be the source of wealth for both individuals and organisations. As we have seen, value comes from, and rewards accrue to, skills and knowledge.

THE TOP 20 SKILLS FOR THE KNOWLEDGE ECONOMY

Brian Phillips of www.seek.co.nz, writing about career management in the knowledge economy, notes that 'employers will seek people who can think, who can research, who love confusion and change, who are flexible and who will be happy – because employers are not sure where we're all headed either.' In the same piece, Phillips identifies the following 'top 20 core skills for a modern economy':

Career planning	Interpersonal skills	Problem-solving
Change management	Marketing	Research
Coaching	Mathematics	Self-management
Computer literacy	Negotiation	Strategic planning
Continuous improvement	Networking	Team leadership
Customer service	Performance management	Writing
Finance	Presentation	

The final point is perhaps an obvious one: as the old certainties of conventional careers are replaced, so will be the trappings that were such effective metrics as signals of success (and, conversely, of failure). No more the need for the Jaguar, the large office, the leather chair, and the golf club membership. The kinds of careers outlined here will rarely follow the conventional path or involve an incremental promotion every year or two. Given this, how will you know if your own career is stalling? The answer is remarkably simple: if you're not learning, you're in trouble.

chapter eight

Getting Started Tomorrow

Option Paralysis: The tendency, when given unlimited choices, to make none.
- DOUGLAS COUPLAND

Just Do It

Two related themes which have run throughout this book are that

- there is no such thing as a successful recipe for knowledge management; and
- the best way to find out what works in your own organisational context is to start small and learn as you go.

By starting small, drawing on the resources already in your organisation, and following the suggestions provided in books like this, the downside risk to such experimentation can easily be limited.

If you have read this far, then we will take it as given that you are convinced there is something in knowledge management for your organisation (and, equally, perhaps something in it for your own career). We now want to end the book by providing a number of simple suggestions about what you can do tomorrow to start managing knowledge. These ideas are deliberately 'low cost' options, hence providing a 'soft entry' into the field of knowledge management.

Educate Staff About the Value of Knowledge
As scarce as truth is, the supply has always been in excess of the demand.
- JOSH BILLINGS

Although we have assumed *you* are convinced there is something in knowledge management, it is much less likely that the rest of the organisation will be. Consequently, the obvious way to get started on knowledge management is by educating the organisation about the value of knowledge sharing. This might initially involve a presentation to key stakeholders and opinion leaders in the organisation, before rolling it out to a wider audience (and, ideally, using those stakeholders and opinion leaders to take the message forward). As we saw in chapter six, this presentation needs to demonstrate the value that knowledge sharing offers to individual staff members (hence addressing the inevitable 'WIIFM' questions at the outset). The example of Ford's communities of practice in chapter five is instructive here: recall that this system worked by having staff share the ideas and practices that they were proud of. Targeting the pride of the workforce is a powerful way to focus knowledge sharing on how much employees have to offer one another. A useful way to do this is through workshop sessions that have staff, in groups, reflect on (i) what they do best, and (ii) how they would do it better in a workplace freed of constraints. This can be combined with educating staff about the contribution their own job makes to the bottom line of the organisation. By linking knowledge sharing to both individual performance *and* the overall performance of the organisation, a start is made on providing staff with a perspective that extends beyond their own 'silos'. Another useful education strategy is to have staff from other organisations that have knowledge management strategies in place talk to your staff about their experiences.

Run a Pilot Four-Phase Project
To strive, to seek, to find, and not to yield.
- ALFRED, LORD TENNYSON

Given the central argument of this book, this suggestion is so self-evident that we feel foolish making it explicit: find a small project and run it through the four-phase process model outlined in chapter six. It doesn't really matter what the justification for this pilot project is. It could be a performance improvement initiative, a way of helping manage change, or even part of a cultural or technological audit. The point is to introduce a project that will enable you to adapt the four-phase I–R–S–A approach to the specific needs (and expectations) of the organisational culture. In other words, this is not the kind of change that can be pursued in the abstract.

The key to creating an effective knowledge-managing culture is to start small, and then allow the success of those (modest) efforts to sell the value of knowledge management to staff. You could even combine this suggestion with the one above (about educating staff on the value of knowledge sharing) by using the four-phase process to *demonstrate* this value to them. To maximise the learning which occurs, ensure the project involves members from throughout the organisation (that is, is cross-functional in composition). However you use the process, ensure that debriefing makes it clear to participants that, whatever it was they learned from participation, it was *because* they participated.

Look for the Easy Gains
The spark that starts the fire is less significant than the conflagration that then takes place.
- STEPHEN DENNING

The best way to introduce any new process or system to an organisation is to look for places where it will produce rewards most readily — opportunities which offer 'low-hanging fruit' — points of least resistance and maximum gain. The reasons for such an approach are simple: to ensure the project succeeds at the outset so those successes can be used to sell the philosophy of the project into the wider organisation. In the words of one of our clients, 'to get the runs on the board'. Beyond these 'runs', the success of the project means you should be able to elicit endorsements from those who participated, to help convince other staff that what is involved is more than mere hyperbole.

One starting point that should deliver these 'easy gains' is the creation of the organisation's knowledge map ('Yellow Pages'), to identify where the knowledge and expertise in the organisation resides and, thus, provide an easy-to-follow mechanism for connecting staff with institutional expertise. As we saw in chapter six, this involves using a 360-degree review process to create a bottom-up model of the expertise on offer in the organisation. Alternatively, another starting point could be with a centralised list of lessons learned from previous projects. This could include checklists of what to do (that is, what worked) and what to avoid (what went wrong), that serve as guidelines for future projects. Such lists provide a structural mechanism for learning from historical experiences in order to assist staff to do the job better next time.

Establish Your Knowledge Management Goals
Brains first, and then Hard Work.
- EEYORE IN A A MILNE, *THE HOUSE AT POOH CORNER*

Although it makes sound operational sense to start a knowledge management pilot project at the point of least resistance (and maximum reward), the real value of knowledge management is strategic rather than operational. Consequently, and in parallel with the project sent to pick the low-hanging fruit, you should start working on identifying the kinds of knowledge that have strategic value to the organisation. In other words, 'you cannot define and manage intellectual assets unless you know what you are trying to do with them' (Stewart, 1999:70). Any organisation seriously contemplating knowledge management should work with its management team to brainstorm questions like: 'What business are we in? What kind of problems do we want to solve? Where do we get the knowledge we need for those solutions?' and 'What mechanisms can we create to ensure the ongoing identification of problems and potential solutions?' The whole point of thinking about knowledge in a strategic way is to move beyond a focus on the organisation's immediate, operational, needs. Consider how knowledge can help you address future changes to your market and the wider business environment (so you can plan for those changes). Finally, on the question of the strategic value of knowledge, be clear that knowledge dates quickly. Consequently, today's knowledge advantage can all too readily become tomorrow's strategic liability. Be clear that 'what we once knew to be important can blind us to new realities and opportunities' (Rumizen, 2002), and make sure it doesn't.

Motivate Staff to Learn and Share

The great end of knowledge is not knowledge but action.
- T H HUXLEY

Having educated staff about the value of knowledge, demonstrated that value by running a pilot four-phase project, and become clear about where knowledge can provide a strategic advantage to the organisation, the next step is to encourage staff to pursue that kind of knowledge. The simplest way to do this is to reward staff for the creation and sharing of knowledge which contributes to achievement of the organisation's goals. Eventually, this should involve incorporating knowledge-sharing behaviours into the heart of your remuneration and promotion systems. In the interim, though, it will be easier to introduce a 'knowledge-sharing' award that complements those existing systems. This should be a regular (perhaps monthly) award that is given to the member of staff (or team) considered to have contributed the most to the creation or sharing of knowledge. Beyond these material rewards, you can start creating a culture where those who create and share knowledge are seen as the new workplace role-models, by having management talk about these efforts wherever possible. Similarly, a notice board situated in a prominent position, or a newsletter, can also be used to reinforce the message that these are behaviours valued by the organisation. The idea is to turn knowledge work into high-status work in the organisation. In the early days of knowledge management, work on those areas where you can most easily build 'mindshare' among staff.

Create Learning Opportunities
It is better to light one candle than curse the darkness.
– ELEANOR ROOSEVELT

Having introduced systems that encourage staff to start sharing and managing knowledge, you then need to introduce methods that provide them with the room to do so. A simple place to start might be introducing cross-functional meetings so that staff from throughout the organisation can formally, and regularly, share their most recent insights. Equally, you could start by creating opportunities for staff to talk and listen to each other informally. This may simply involve spending more time around the water-cooler and coffee machines, or it may involve something more ambitious, such as the creation of a 'talk room' or a regular knowledge fair. Finally, you could introduce formal mentoring and 'buddying' structures (which are especially valuable where they occur across, as well as within, functional areas). Note that creating the 'space' for staff to share and manage knowledge also means creating the time for them to do so. You need to think about how you can overcome that classic catch-22 of organisational life, 'that employees are too busy working to take time to learn things that will help them work more efficiently' (Davenport and Prusak, 1998:47).

Adapt Your Current IT Systems to Manage Knowledge
The thing with high-tech is that you always end up using scissors.
– DAVID HOCKNEY

Having a supportive IT system in place is a key dimension to successful knowledge management. But rather than thinking about creating a new system with this goal in mind, start by thinking about how you can exploit the existing system to better support a knowledge-managing culture. For instance, think about the way existing client databases, e-mail-based user groups, websites, and groupware could be adapted to enable better knowledge-sharing. One way forward here is to reconsider how those systems are managed. We recently worked with a client whose problem was that the intranet was becoming unusable because staff were simply putting all their files into the 'work in progress' directory (and, more importantly, not taking them out of that directory when the project was complete). As a consequence, nobody other than the person working on a particular project knew where to find the relevant files. Given that this is the knowledge management consultant's worst nightmare, we came up with the simplest solution imaginable – give the database manager sole responsibility for managing the system's directory structure. Staff were still able to add and edit content, but by having only one person responsible for structuring the directory tree, the client quickly regained a useful, location-addressable, file-management system.

Beyond questions of how the IT system is managed, there are usually efficiency gains available through training staff to use the existing functionality better. Educating staff how to use existing systems better is 'a powerful but under utilized' knowledge-management tool (Davenport and Beck, 2001:102). As with all the learning discussed in this book, this 'education' can be both formalised training and informal peer-led learning. To cite another example from our own experience: we recently worked with an organisation where the only person who could add or edit content in the database was the database manager. Changing the system to enable all staff to be able to do these things was an obvious step forward, but doing so first meant staff had to be trained in (i) how to make an entry or edit one, (ii) how to summarise their own experiences succinctly, and (iii) what counted as useful or trivial content.

HELP MENUS, HELP DESKS, AND NO HELP AT ALL

How much training do staff in your organisation receive about how to use the computer system? If industry norms are anything to go by, probably not much at all. One study carried out by Outsell discovered that two-thirds of those staff who use the Web for 'research' had never received any formal training about what to do; over half of the workers surveyed had never received any formal computer training at all; and only 18% of respondents had ever received more than eight hours' training. But, most interesting of all, despite this lack of training, 96 per cent of those surveyed considered themselves 'skilled' or 'very adept' at finding information (cited in Davenport and Beck, 2001:202).

KNOWLEDGE MANAGEMENT

Experiment With Novel Ways of Sharing Knowledge

'The time has come' the Walrus said, 'To talk of many things:
'Of shoes and ships and sealing wax — Of cabbages and kings
And why the sea is boiling hot — And whether pigs have wings.'
– LEWIS CARROLL, THROUGH THE LOOKING GLASS

The logic of our four-phase model is straightforward: you identify where the knowledge resides in your organisation; reflect on what it is that you know; share that knowledge with whoever needs to know it; and then apply that knowledge to change the way people do things in the organisation. Given this, we can see that knowledge management is about transforming knowledge into action. Achieving this transformation demands the effective communication of knowledge between those we have elsewhere called the 'sellers' and 'buyers' of that knowledge. But how do you ensure that effective communication occurs? We have argued that this relies on two distinct components. The first is that the knowledge-sharing system (in the broadest possible sense) is designed so 'buyers' actively go in search of the knowledge needed to answer their questions. By having the 'buyers' pull the information they need from the organisational memory, you can be assured that they will be motivated to pay attention to what is communicated (after all, they expended the effort to go in search of it). The second component of effective communication is that the messages communicated through the knowledge-sharing system engage the attention of the buyers. In this book, we have talked about the value that storytelling, learning narratives, metaphors, telling jokes, knowledge fairs, and 'memos as newspaper headlines' have. These unconventional methods of communication work because they cut through the clutter of traditional organisational communication (the standard procedure manuals, memos, and reports that spend most of their lives as shelfware). Undoubtedly, there will be some resistance to these novel ways of sharing knowledge in your organisation, so why not create some in-house experiments to discover what kinds of methods work well in your culture? If nothing else, this offers a guaranteed way to have some fun. Think about what novel forums you could use, what novel methods, and what novel settings. When we were academics, and had to waste inordinate amounts of time stuck in pointless departmental meetings, we used to imagine how much more effective those meetings would be if we just held them standing up in the hallways. Unfortunately, whenever we suggested it, our professors thought we were joking. The larger point here is that we have all been told that the key to communicating anything important is to 'keep it simple [and] stupid' (KISS). But in the knowledge economy, what Thomas Davenport and John Beck describe as 'the Attention Economy', what really matters is that you 'make it novel [and] timely' (MINT). And to paraphrase the *Smint* ads, 'No MINT, no KISS.'

Demonstrate that It Is Paying Its Way
'Show me the money!'
- JERRY MCGUIRE

The international research evidence clearly demonstrates that the benefits of creating a healthy knowledge-management culture are substantial. Productivity increases, organisations become more innovative, and they become more flexible in dealing with change (and especially in responding to crises). In addition, workplace morale improves, there is a greater sense of organisational coherence, and knowledge-stocks increase. The good news is that the evidence for these rewards should make selling your own knowledge management initiative to senior management easier. However, if you promise these (or any such) rewards then you will also need to create mechanisms that enable you to demonstrate their achievement. In other words, all knowledge management initiatives need evaluation and monitoring systems that enable you to see how (and where) the initiative is adding value. Given that you will want to argue for a change in these metrics over time (*improved* performance, *increased* innovation, *better* able to respond to crises, etc.), some kind of benchmarking design will be required. Although there are a number of interim 'knowledge sharing' metrics that you could adopt (see our notes on Skandia's 'Navigator' in chapter two), we think the goal here should focus on demonstrating the desired outcomes rather than the interim inputs.

THE PRECONDITIONS FOR BENCHMARKING

Benchmarking is a powerful mechanism for assessing the effects of organisational change. But to provide a valid measure of those effects, a number of preconditions need to be fulfilled. Benchmarking comparisons require that

- the measures taken across time measure the same effect;
- the moment in time when the change occurred is discrete, and easily identified;
- any 'effects' seen can be legitimately attributed to the change; and
- it is possible to distil the effects of the change from broader changes going on at the same time (attribution effects and biases).

KNOWLEDGE MANAGEMENT

Leading from the Front?
'Forward!' he cried, from the rear. And the front rank died.
– PINK FLOYD, 'US AND THEM'

One of the questions we are often asked is 'Do we need a chief knowledge officer (CKO) to manage knowledge?' Our answer, invariably, is 'Not in the early days.' Given that we are firm believers in the need to start small, it is hard to see how a CKO can be of much help. That said, there is no reason why the manager of the initial knowledge management project could not evolve into a CKO over time. Instead of a CKO, what we think is required in the early days of knowledge management is that as many managers as possible (along with key opinion leaders among the staff) are seen to support and model knowledge-sharing behaviours. This means moving beyond gaining a vague sense of their 'buy in', to an organisation where those managers (and opinion leaders) actively integrate knowledge sharing into their day-to-day operations.

A Brief Word on What Not to Do

Pay no attention to what critics say.
No statue has ever been put up to a critic.
– JEAN SIBELIUS

Earlier drafts of this chapter contained long lists of 'traps for young players'. However, we edited those out of the later versions when we realised they were simply the converse of the suggestions we have provided above. Instead, we have left in the five most common mistakes that we think organisations make when starting out with knowledge management:

- ○ starting out before they are clear about how knowledge contributes to the organisation's strategic goals. Many organisations pursue knowledge management because it sounds like a good idea, or because it is fashionable, or because some influential manager heard about the idea from a friend or colleague, but without really thinking through how it will integrate with the broader organisational impetus. Consequently, knowledge management becomes simply another organisational initiative competing for the attention of staff.

- starting out without really understanding how knowledge management works or what is involved. This inevitably means underestimating the degree of organisational change involved in driving knowledge-sharing to the heart of the organisation. The idea that 'knowledge' has become the pre-eminent source of competitive advantage runs the risk of being reduced to a 'motherhood and apple pie' statement (one that nobody would ever dispute). But what are you prepared to give up in order to achieve it?
- starting out before being clear about the methods needed to ensure knowledge creation and sharing occurs in the organisation. Precisely because there is no-one recipe for successful knowledge management, organisations need to develop personalised approaches that reflect the reality (and expectations) of their own cultures. We believe this means knowledge management is really all about (i) starting small, (ii) experimenting, and (iii) creating systems based on the evidence of past successes.
- putting too much faith in computers. We have talked about this at length throughout the book and so do not want to belabour the point here. We just want to reiterate that (i) knowledge management is all about learning and computers never learn, only people do, and (ii) if the organisation allocates more than one-third of a knowledge management project's resources to information technology then it is no longer a knowledge management project.
- putting too much faith in consultants. At the risk of alienating colleagues everywhere, we think organisations put too much faith in (and accord too much prominence to) consultants. Although consultants can certainly help guide the successful introduction of knowledge management, it is important to distinguish between general and specific advice. Left to their own devices, consultants are likely to create systems that are divorced from the day-to-day realities of those that have to work with them because consultants can only ever have a limited insight into how people actually do their job (or even how the organisation works). Knowledge management needs to be driven by what sociologists call 'working knowledge' — and the only people who have access to that are those who do the work. The lesson, then, is that knowledge management systems are likely to work best where the people who generate the knowledge are also those who store it, explain it to others, and coach them as they try to apply it.

Conclusion

So where does this leave us? We want to finish this book by reiterating that knowledge management, in its broadest sense, is not simply another fad. If anything, it provides an opportunity to bring together many of the established, smart, ways of working to respond to the new world of business. If the phrases hadn't been emptied of all credibility by over-use (and abuse), we could simply say that knowledge management is all about working smarter, through the empowerment of staff via learning. Think of it as 'intelligence in action', but the collective intelligence of the entire organisation, irrespective of where it resides or what it looks like.

In the end, knowledge management comes down to recognising that the experiences and ideas of the staff in any organisation provide a crucial source of competitive advantage. Tapping that source of advantage is about creating an organisation where staff can learn from one another and feel encouraged to do so, and where all staff understand the relationship between individual, team, and organisational performance. In a world of increasingly scarce human resources, knowledge management is about attracting the right people, keeping them challenged, treating them well, and allowing them to shape part of the organisation in their own image. And when we put it like that, it doesn't sound like such a bad idea at all.

We'll leave the last words to that Maori proverb we quoted in chapter three:

> *Ask me what is the most important thing*
> *And I will reply*
> *It is people,*
> *It is people,*
> *It is people.*

Notes

1. We should perhaps note that the label 'knowledge management' is indeed a curious one to the extent that what is involved is not the management of knowledge per se but the use of it. In this regard knowledge management is similar to time management in that you don't ever manage time but only how you and your staff use it.
2. Baruch Lev is the Philip Bardes Professor of Accounting and Finance at New York University, Stern School of Business, the Director of the Vincent C. Ross Institute for Accounting Research and the Project for Research on Intangibles.
3. Although Skandia's critical leadership in this area is well established, it was 'only just' the leader: Dow Chemicals, Hughes Aircraft, and the Canadian Imperial Bank of Commerce all also started early and figure prominently in the literature.
4. We didn't when we discovered that the original poem is over 30 pages long – prompting one of our research assistants to ask 'Where is the audience you have lost in verbosity?'
5. Quinn et al. argue that, although there is a burgeoning literature in the area of knowledge, very little specifically addresses the question of managing professional intellect. They write 'this oversight is especially surprising because professional intellect creates most of the value in the new economy.' (Quinn et al, 1998:182)
6. We haven't reached the 'care why' phase, so we're not yet in a position to talk about what it looks like. But as soon as we come up with an innovative alternative to focus groups, you'll be able to read about it in our copyright application.
7. One description of path dependency that we really like comes from www.korpios.org: 'Path dependency is like a cheetah sprinting full speed after an antelope. Out of the corner of its eye, the cheetah may see even bigger game, but it's already barrelling after the smaller one, and changing course would require enormous energy. Therefore it's easier just to continue in the same direction.'
8. Which reminds us of the joke about the two economists discussing the Napoleonic

wars over lunch. One turns to the other and says 'What do you think the impact of those wars was on the economic growth of Europe?' The other wipes his mouth and answers 'Too early to tell.'

9. As one of our colleagues put it, the fact that there is any argument here at all is compelling evidence of the failure of IT. The whole promise of the technology was that it would change our lives in ways that would be overwhelming, not that we would have to search for those benefits with a magnifying glass and in-depth econometric analyses.

10. As social scientists, we feel compelled to point out that this creates an ever-increasing gap between the knowledge-rich and the knowledge-poor. This is the 'winner-take-all society' that Robert Frank and Philip Cook (1996) write about, something that is also known as the 'hollowing out' of society. Left to its own devices, the knowledge economy is indeed one where the (knowledge) rich get richer and the (knowledge) poor get poorer. Undoubtedly, such a divergence will have drastic consequences for the future of our societies if not addressed. One school of thought is that public investment in education and R&D will make everyone knowledge rich, and hence able to participate in the knowledge economy. Another is simply that the market will resolve this problem precisely because 'when educated workers get bigger paychecks, fewer people [will] stay uneducated.' (Stewart, 1999:47). We are not convinced.

A Knowledge Management Glossary

AAR: after action review. A structured debrief built in to the life-cycle of a project, in order for participants to review what was learned from the project.

Bandwidth: a measure of the capacity to transfer data. More is better.

Beta test: a field test of a prototype version of a product (such as software), especially by testers outside the company developing it, that is conducted prior to its commercial release.

Bot: (from *roBOT*): a semi-automated program, such as one which indexes web pages or sorts e-mail.

Browser: a programme used for viewing web pages.

CFO: chief financial officer.

Change agent: someone responsible for planning and implementing an organisational change. As knowledge management initiatives are also fundamentally change management initiatives, change agents are an important component of successful knowledge management.

Change management: the field that focuses on the techniques used to implement change. Sometimes also called 'change leadership' to highlight the fact that such processes should 'lead' rather than simply 'manage' change.

Cephalisation (and **decephalisation**): the approach to decision making found in traditional hierarchical organisations where decisions have to be referred to the 'head' of the unit or organisation. Decephalisation is the tendency to overcome this approach.

CIO: chief information officer.

CKO: nothing to do with a TKO, CKO stands for chief knowledge officer – the senior executive responsible for leveraging knowledge in an organisation. CKOs work with, and are at the same level of seniority as, the organisation's CIO.

CLO: chief learning officer. An alternative label for the CKO, albeit usually in those organisations that have a tendency to focus on the human resource aspects of knowledge management (that is, learning).

Codification: an approach to knowledge management that concentrates on ways to codify and store knowledge. Such knowledge management initiatives tend to be information technology-intensive.

Communities of practice: tightknit groups formed by people working together on the same, or similar, tasks. A key component of knowledge management because of the role such communities play in creating and transferring knowledge.

Connectors: in Malcolm Gladwell's memorable phrase, connectors are 'people with a special gift for bringing the world together' (2000:38). In knowledge management, they are sometimes known as 'knowledge brokers', the kind of people who can find the person with the answer to your knowledge need.

Content maps: a high-level description that summarises and organises the meaning contained in a collection of electronic documents.

Corporate amnesia: the loss of collective experience, knowledge, and skills from an organisation, usually due to staff turnover or change initiatives.

Corporate memory: the collective experience, knowledge, and skills that exist in an organisation. As with individuals, organisations can be made to remember their past (and, in best case examples, even learn from it).

Critical success factor(s): the prior condition(s) that must be fulfilled before the intended goal can be achieved.

CRM: Customer Relationship Management. Solutions and strategies for managing businesses' relationships with customers. In practice, many CRM systems are simply elaborate contacts databases.

Customer capital: the value that results from the relationships an organisation has with its customers.

Database: an electronic store of data and information.

Discontinuity of knowledge: what occurs when experienced knowledge workers move from one job to another without first transferring their knowledge to their co-workers.

DNA: define, nurture, allocate (see chapter seven).

E-commerce: electronic commerce. Business carried out over the Internet. The two major forms of e-commerce are Business-to-Consumer (B2C) and Business-to-Business (B2B). The terms 'e-business' and 'e-tailing' are often used synonymously with e-commerce.

Employee competence: the capabilities of your staff. Sometimes used to describe what we have called knowledge.

ERP: Enterprise Resource Planning system. A centralised system that enables organisations to keep informed about, and in control of, their production and business processes. In practice, many ERP systems are merely fancy accounting systems.

EVA: Economic Value Added. A financial performance measure that estimates the true 'economic' profit of an enterprise, or the amount by which earnings exceed, or fall short of, the required minimum rate of return that shareholders and lenders could get by investing in other securities of comparable risk.

Externalisation: the transfer of knowledge from the minds of staff members to an external store of some kind. Externalisation describes the process by which tacit knowledge is made explicit.

Extranet: an extension of an organisation's intranet to make it available to selected outsiders (such as some customers, suppliers, partners, etc.).

FAQs: frequently asked questions. A resource that provides answers to common problems and questions.

Friction points: points (and sites) of resistance to a change initiative.

GIGO: 'garbage in, garbage out'. A cautionary warning that any piece of information technology is only ever as good as the quality of the data and information fed into it.

Groupware: software that enables groups of people to work collaboratively on the same project. Also called 'teamware'.

Human capital: the collective value of the know-how held by an organisation's staff.

Informal organisation: how things actually get done in any organisation. The informal, improvisational practices that keep organisations functioning. Seen most clearly in the difference between what the formal job description says a staff member *should* be doing and what they *actually* do all day.

Intangible assets: things that have a value to the organisaton but have no physical presence. In the knowledge economy, intangible assets are your organisation's 'unbearable lightness of being'.

Intellectual capital: the collective value of the knowledge assets available to an organisation (comprising human, structural, and customer/supplier capital).

Intellectual property: that subset of intellectual capital that can be protected by law.

Internalisation: the transfer of knowledge from an external store into the minds of staff. Internalisation is how explicit knowledge is transformed into tacit knowledge. Also known as learning.

Intranet: an organisation's internal computer network. Intranets provide a common way that organisations share data and information with, and among, their staff.

IPO: initial public (share-) offering. Also known as a share market 'float'.

IT: information technology or technologies.

JIC: just in case (method of maintaining inventory that called for larger stocks in case they were needed).

JIT: just in time (method of controlling inventory so that stock is available when it is needed, not before).

Kaizen: continuous incremental improvement.

Kanban: an index card used in a JIT parts-ordering system.

Killer app: the 'killer application'. Programmes that you simply have to have. See 'vapourware'.

Knowledge exchange: a type of database where staff are able to add their own ideas as well as use those of others.

Knowledge half-life: the point at which the acquisition of new knowledge becomes more cost-effective and offers greater returns than the maintenance of existing knowledge.

Knowledge map: a tool for identifying where the key areas of expertise in an organisation reside.

Knowledge workers: in a knowledge economy, your staff will be 'hired minds' far more than 'hired hands'. Because they are hired for their capacity to learn and teach (that is, to share what they know), it is imperative that organisations keep them learning.

LAN: local area network. A computer network limited to a single building or small area, designed so employees can share information. (LANs are Ethernet-based systems, running software from Novell or Oracle.)

Learning community: an informal group of people that crosses organisational boundaries and comes together to discuss issues of interest.

Learning organisation: an organisation with the requisite processes and culture to promote continuous learning.

Metadata: a summary of existing data, often providing context, in order to make it more useful (and useable).

Network of practice: like a 'community of practice', a 'network of practice' is a network that links people to others who work on similar practices. Unlike a 'community of practice' (which is tightknit), the members of a 'network of practice' may never meet one another and simply 'network' at a distance.

Newbie: a 'new beginner'. Internet slang for someone who hasn't been using computers or the Internet long.

Newsgroup: a discussion group based on postings by members on a particular topic. The groups can be either 'moderated', where someone decides which postings will become part of the discussion, or 'unmoderated', where everything posted is included in the discussion.

Netiquette: Internet etiquette. The unwritten rules about what is acceptable when using e-mail, online chat groups, and newsgroups.

NIH: not invented here. Syndrome characterised by individuals or organisations refusing to use a technology that they didn't create themselves.

PDA: personal digital assistant.

PDF: Portable Document Format. A file format developed by Adobe Corporation to allow the efficient electronic distribution of large documents. A PDF file will look the same on the screen and in print regardless of what kind of computer you are using or which software package was used to create it.

Personalisation: an approach to knowledge management that involves retrieving and structuring knowledge to best meet the preferences (and skills) of staff members.

Portal: a website that acts as a starting point for many other sites. Common portals include Google, Yahoo, Netscape, and so on.

Search engine: a website directory which indexes as many websites as it can and allows you to search its database for sites on particular subjects.

Shareware: software that you can use for a limited period of time before having to pay for it. This enables you to fully evaluate it before you purchase.

Skunk works: a small, specialised department or facility, that functions with minimal supervision within a company, producing ideas or experimental designs.

Socialisation: bringing together staff who work on similar practices, to enable the sharing of tacit knowledge.

Spam: junk e-mail.

Springboard story: a story that engages the audience and achieves a shift in understanding about possible outcomes or paths forward.

SQL: Structured Query Language. The standard expressions (language) used for accessing and modifying information in a database.

Structural capital: the value of an organisation's systems, processes, and policies. The things that translate human capital into useful products and services.

Systems thinking: conventional problem-solving reduces a problem to its constituent parts and deals with those parts in isolation. Systems thinking deals with the problem (and the problem situation) holistically. Here, the whole is recognised as being more than a sum of the parts.

Tacit knowledge: things your staff know that they do not know they know (or do not know how to externalise). For instance, how are you able to make sense of this definition?

Taxonomy: a framework to structure knowledge with. An index is a common example of a taxonomy. Taxonomies help users understand how knowledge can be grouped together. A way of classifying things.

Text editor: any word processing programme that enables you to type and edit text.

TQM: total quality management. A structured system designed to continuously improve the performance of organisational processes in order to satisfy internal and external customers and suppliers.

Triple bottom line: the organisation measures itself according to not just its financial performance but also its contribution to the environment and society. The notion of reporting against the three 'bottom lines' of economic, environmental, and social performance is tied to the goal of sustainable development.

URL: Uniform Resource Locator. The address of a certain file or directory on the Web. For instance, http://www.nodoubt.co.nz is the URL for our company's web site.

Value network: a web of relationships that generates tangible value through complex changes of intangibles.

Vapourware: a derogatory term for software which is announced but fails to materialise (see 'killer app').

Website: a collection of web pages.

WIIFM: depending on whom you listen to, WIIFM is either the 'easy listening' of change management or its 'greatest hits'. It is short for 'What's in it for me?' and describes a common response to any change initiative.

XML: Extensible Markup Language. A web development format for defining specialised markup languages.

YMMV: 'Your mileage may vary'. Internet slang, meaning 'Your experience may be different'. Derives from the standard disclaimer used in car ads regarding claimed economy figures.

References

Argyris, C. (1998) 'Teaching Smart People How to Learn'. In *Harvard Business Review on Knowledge Management*. Harvard Business School Press.

Austin, R. (2001) 'Hotshot Envy: The Trials and Tribulations of Managing Smart People'. *WEB business*. June/July 2001. 4:50.

Bamford, J. (2001) *Body of Secrets: Anatomy of the Ultra-Secret National Security Agency*. Doubleday, New York.

Barber, B. R. (1996) *Jihad vs. McWorld: How Globalism and Tribalism are Reshaping the World*. Ballantine Books, New York.

Boulding, K. (1956) 'General Systems Theory: The Skeleton of Science'. *Management Science*. April 1956. 2 (3).

Bourdieu, P. (1996) *On Television*. The New Press, New York.

Boyle, D. (2000) *The Tyranny of Numbers: Why Counting Can't Make Us Happy*. Harper Collins, London.

Brown, J. S. and Duguid, P. (2000) *The Social Life of Information*. Harvard Business School Press, Boston, Mass.

Bryson, B. (1987) *Troublesome Words*. Second Edition. Penguin, London.

Burke, J. (1985) *The Day The Universe Changed*. Little, Brown and Company, Boston.

Calder, P. (2001) 'Innovate, Don't Imitate'. *Weekend Herald*. 21–22 July 2001. B4.

Carlile, P. R. (1998) 'Working Knowledge: How Organizations Manage What They Know'. *Human Resource Planning*. 21(4): 58–59.

Chalmers, A. (1982) *What is this thing called Science?* Second Edition. Open University Press, Milton Keynes.

Cowey, M. (2000) 'Knowledge: Fact or Fad?' *Management*. May 2000. 54–55.

CPUniverse.com (2001) 'Young People Stupid: Technology at Fault'. *CPUniverse.com's Weekly Review*. 5 February 2001.

Davenport, T. H. and Beck, J. C. (2001) *The Attention Economy: Understanding the New Currency of Business*. Harvard Business School Press, Boston, Mass.

Davenport, T. H; De Long, D. W; and Beers, M. C. (1998) 'Successful Knowledge Management Projects'. *Sloan Management Review*. Winter 1998. 43–57.

Davenport, T. H. and Prusak, L. (1998) *Working Knowledge: How Organizations Manage What They Know*. Harvard Business School Press, Boston, Mass.

Davidson, C. (2000) 'Confessions from a BFR (Bungled Flight Review?)' *Pacific Wings*. February 2000. 37.

Davidson, C. (1999) 'Whatever you have to pay for it (or, Dodging Clouds and Chasing Sunsets)'. *New Zealand Sport Flying*. Spring 1999. 8–9.

Davidson, C (1997) 'Learning about Spinning'. *Pilot*. April 1997. 31 (4):60–61. London, England.

Dawson, G. (2000) *Life Is So Good*. HarperCollins, Sydney, Australia (with Richard Glaubman).

De Botton, A. (1997) *How Proust Can Change Your Life*. Picador, London.

Denning, S. (2001) *The Springboard: How Storytelling Ignites Action in Knowledge-Era Organizations*. Butterworth-Heinemann. October 2000.

Dertouzos, M. L; Lester, R. K; Solow, R. M. (1989) *Made in America*. MIT Press, Cambridge, Mass.

Dilllman, D. A. (1978) *Mail and Telephone Surveys: The Total Design Method*. John Wiley and Sons, New York.

Doder, D. (2001) 'We're All Ears'. *The Nation*. June 18 2001. 272 (24):25–29.

Drucker, P. (1998) 'The Coming of the New Organization'. In *Harvard Business Review on Knowledge Management*. Harvard Business School Publishing.

Drucker, P. (1997) *Managing in a Time of Great Change*. Butterworth-Heinemann, Oxford.

Edvinsson, L. and Malone, M. S. (1997) *Intellectual Capital: The Proven Way to Establish Your Company's Real Value by Measuring its Hidden Brainpower*. Piatkus, London [also HarperBusiness, HarperCollins Inc. in the USA].

Ernst and Young (1999) *The Knowledge Economy*. Submission to the New Zealand Government by the Minister for Information Technology's IT Advisory Group, Wellington, August 1999.

Evans, P. and Wurster, T. S. (2000) *Blown to Bits: How the New Economics of Information Transforms Strategy*. Harvard Business School Press, Boston, Mass.

Ewing, R. (2001) 'Doing what comes naturally – 'naturalistic' decision making. *Pacific Wings*. May/June 2000. 33.

Fallows, J. (1997) *Breaking the News: How the Media Undermine American Democracy*. Vintage Books, New York.

Frank, R. H. and Cook, P. J. (1996) *The Winner-Take-All Society: Why the Few at the Top Get So Much More Than the Rest of Us*. Penguin, New York.

Friedman, T. (1999) *The Lexus and the Olive Tree: Fast Food, Fanaticism – the World We Live in Today*. HarperCollins, New York.

Fukuyama, F. (1996) *Trust: The Social Virtues and the Creation of Prosperity*. Free Press Paperbacks, New York.

Gardner, H. (1983) *Frames of Mind: The Theory of Multiple Intelligences*. Basic Books, New York.

Garvin, D. (1998) 'Building a Learning Organization'. In *Harvard Business Review on Knowledge Management*. Harvard Business School Publishing.

REFERENCES

Gates, B. [with Hemmingway, C.] (1999) *Business at the Speed of Thought: Using a Digital Nervous System*. Penguin, London.

Giddens, A. (1998) *The Third Way: The Renewal of Social Democracy*. Polity Press, Cambridge.

Gladwell, M. (2000) *The Tipping Point: How Little Things Can Make a Big Difference*. Little Brown and Company, New York.

Gleick, J. (1999) *Faster: The Acceleration of Just About Everything*. Pantheon Books, New York.

Gleick, J. (1987) *Chaos: Making a New Science*. Penguin Books, London.

Gordon, J. (1999) 'Intellectual Capital and You'. *Training*. September 1999. 36(9): 30–38.

Hamel, G. (2000) *Leading the Revolution*. Harvard Business School Press, Boston, Mass.

Handy, C. (1995) *The Empty Raincoat: Making Sense of the Future*. Arrow Books, London.

Handy, C. (1990) *The Age of Unreason*. Arrow Books. London.

Heck, M. (1999) '"DocuShare" Handles Large Data Collections'. *InfoWorld*. 7 June 1999. 21(23).

Hewitt, P. (2000) 'Creating Competitive Advantage in the Knowledge Economy'. A speech given at the Said Business School, Oxford University, 21 November 2000.

Hilderband, C. (1999) 'KM Gets Real'. *CIO Magazine*, from http://www.cio.com, posted 30 December 1999.

Hobsbawm, E. (2000) *The New Century*. Little, Brown, and Company, London.

Hood, M. (2000) 'Microsoft races to plug a brain drain'. *The New Zealand Herald*. 12 June 2000.

Information Technology Advisory Group (ITAG) (1999) *The Knowledge Economy*, submission to the New Zealand Government by the Minister for Information Technology's IT Advisory Group, Wellington, August 1999.

Iyer, P. (2000) *The Global Soul: Jet Lag, Shopping Malls, and the Search for More*. Bloomsbury, London.

Jayne, V. (2001a) 'HR, not IT, is the key to knowledge'. *New Zealand Herald*. 4 July 2001. D1.

Jayne, V. (2001b) 'Clearly, sofas are a winner'. *New Zealand Herald*. 8 August 2001. D1.

Johnson, S. (1998) *Who Moved My Cheese?* Vermilion, London.

Jonscher, C. (2000) *Wired Life: Who are we in the digital age?* Anchor (Transworld Publishers), Random House, London.

Ketz, J. (2001) 'The Accounting Cycle: Wash, Rinse, and Spin (Oh, the Intangibility of Intangibles!)'. http://accounting.smartpros.com/x29141.xml

Kim, W. C. and Mauborgne, R. (1997) 'Fair Process: Managing in the Knowledge Economy'. *Harvard Business Review*. July–August 1997. 65–75.

Klleiner, A. and Roth, G. (1998) 'How to Make Experience Your Company's Best Teacher'. In *Harvard Business Review on Knowledge Management*. Harvard Business School Publishing.

Knowledge Management News (e-newsletter): www.kmnews.com

Kouloupoulos, T. and Frappaolo, C. (1999) *Smart Things to Know About Knowledge Management.* Capstone Publishing, Oxford.

Leadbeater, C. (2000) *Living on Thin Air.* Penguin Books, London.

Leonard, D. and Straus, S. (1998) 'Putting Your Company's Whole Brain to Work'. In *Harvard Business Review on Knowledge Management.* Harvard Business School Publishing.

Lewis, M. (2000) *The New New Thing: A Silicon Valley Story.* Hodder and Stoughton, London.

Locke, J. (1998) *The De-Voicing of Society: Why We Don't Talk to Each Other Anymore.* Simon and Schuster, New York.

Mandow, N. (2001) 'A Boss to Die For'. *Unlimited.* 1 May 2001.

Marshall, G. (ed.) (1994) *The Concise Oxford Dictionary of Sociology.* Oxford University Press, Oxford.

Mingo, J. (1994) *How the Cadillac Got Its Fins: And Other Tales from the Annals of Business and Marketing.* Harper Business, New York.

Nonaka, I. (1998) 'The Knowledge-Creating Company'. In *Harvard Business Review on Knowledge Management.* Harvard Business School Publishing.

New Hamlyn Encyclopedic World Dictionary (1988) Paul Hamlyn, London.

NZ Business (2001) 'The email deluge'. *NZ Business.* June 2001. 5.

OECD (1996) *The Knowledge Based Economy.* Paper presented at the OECD, Paris. [Cited in Rollo and Clarke, 2001:4].

Pan, S. L. (1999) 'Knowledge management in practice: An exploratory case study'. *Technology Analysis and Strategic Management.* September 1999. 11(3): 359–374.

Pan, S. L. and Scarborough, H. (1998) 'A socio-technical view of knowledge sharing at Buckman Laboratories'. *Journal of Knowledge Management.* September 1998. 2(1):55–66.

Parker, I. (2001) 'Absolute PowerPoint'. *The New Yorker.* 28 May 2001. 76–87.

Parker, S. (2000) 'Catchword is integrity in modern workplace', *New Zealand Herald*, February 9 2000, D1.

Penzias, A. (1989) *Ideas and Information.* Touchstone, Simon and Schuster, New York.

Perry, M.; Davidson, C.; and Hill, R. (1995) *Reform at Work: Workplace Change and the New Industrial Order.* Longman Paul, Auckland.

Pfeffer, J. and Sutton, R. I. (2000) *The Knowing–Doing Gap: How Smart Companies Turn Knowledge into Action.* Harvard Business School Press, Boston, Mass.

Pfeffer, J. and Sutton, R. I. (1999) 'Knowing what to do is not enough: Turning knowledge into action'. *California Management Review.* Fall 1999. 42(1): 83–108.

Phillips, B. (1998) 'The Top 20 Skills'. http://www.seek.co.nz/editorial/0-2-1_20_skills.htm

Philp, M. (2001) 'Surf's Up'. *The Listener.* 4 August 2001. 26–27. Auckland, New Zealand.

Polanyi, M. (1958) *Personal knowledge: Towards a post-critical philosophy.* Routledge & Kegan Paul, London.

Pratkanis, A. and Aronson, E. (2000) *Age of Propaganda: The Everyday Use and Abuse of Persuasion*. W. H. Freeman and Company. New York.

Quinn, J. B. (1999) 'Strategic outsourcing: Leveraging knowledge capabilities'. *Sloan Management Review.* Summer 1999. 40(4): 9–21.

Quinn, J. B; Anderson, P. and Finkelstein, S. (1998) 'Managing Professional Intellect: Making the Most of the Best'. In *Harvard Business Review on Knowledge Management.* Harvard Business School Publishing.

Raman, V. (2001) 'Knowledge economy should revisit education'. *The National Business Review.* 16 November 2001. 46.

Reich, R. (1992) *The Work of Nations.* Vintage Books, New York.

Reuters (1997) *Dying for Information?* Reuters Business Information (from http://www.cni.org/regconfs/1997/ukoln-content/repor~13.html).

Richardson, M. (2001) 'The Knowledge Economy ... no more business as usual'. *University of Auckland Business Review.* 3 (1):37–46.

Ritzer, G (1996) *The McDonaldization of Society: An Investigation into The Changing Character of Contemporary Social Life.* Pine Forge Press, Thousand Oaks, California.

Rollo, C. and Clarke, T. (2001) *International Best Practice: Case Studies in Knowledge Management.* Standards Australia HB275 Supplement 1, Sydney.

Roszak, T. (1986) *The Cult of Information: The Folklore of Computers and the True Art of Thinking.* Pantheon Books, New York.

Rumizen, M. C. (2002) *The Complete Idiot's Guide to Knowledge Management.* Alpha Books, Indianapolis.

Rushkoff, D. (1999) *Coercion: The Persuasion Professionals and Why We Listen to What They Say.* Little, Brown, and Company, London.

Rybczynski, R. (1983) *Taming the Tiger: The Struggle to Control Technology.* Penguin, New York.

Saul, J. R. (1997) *The Unconscious Civilization.* Penguin Books, Harmondsworth, Middlesex.

Saul, J. R. (1993) *Voltaire's Bastards: The Dictatorship of Reason in the West.* Vintage Books, New York.

Schor, J. B. (1991) *The Overworked American: The Unexpected Decline of Leisure.* Basic Books, New York.

Scherer, K. (2001) 'Knowledge as a power tool'. *New Zealand Herald.* 27 July 2001. C7.

Seglin, J. L. (2000) 'Storytelling only works if tales are true'. *The New York Times.* 19 November 2000.

Semler, R. (1994) *Maverick.* Arrow, Random House, London.

Sennet, R. (1998) *The Corrosion of Character: The Personal Consequences of Work in the New Capitalism.* W. W. Norton and Company, New York.

Shenk, D. (1997) *Data Smog: Surviving the Information Glut.* Abacus, London.

Shorris, E. (1994) *A Nation of Salesmen: The Tyranny of the Market and the Subversion of Culture.* Avon Books, New York.

Stamps, D. (1999) 'Is Knowledge Management a Fad?' *Training.* March 1999. 36 (3):36–42.

Standards Australia (2001) *International Best Practice: Case Studies in Knowledge Management.* Standards Australia HB275 Supplement 1, Sydney.

Stewart, T. (2001) 'You Think Your Company's So Smart? Prove It'. *Fortune.* 30 April 2001. 105.

Stewart, T. (1999) *Intellectual Capital: The New Wealth of Organizations.* Currency Books, New York.

Tapsell, S. (2001) 'Harnessing knowledge with intranets'. *Management.* July 2001. 36–40.

Tenner, E. (1997) *Why Things Bite Back: Technology and the Revenge of Unintended Consequences.* Vintage, New York.

Toutonghi, P. (2000) *Market Capitalization and Expenditure Capitalization,* smartpros.com, 4 December, 2000. http://accounting.smartpros.com/x27548.xml

Webber, A. M. (2000) 'New Math for a New Economy'. *Fast Company.* January–February 2000. 31:214.

Winch, P. (1958) *The Idea Of A Social Science: And its Relation to Philosophy.* Routledge and Kegan Paul, London.

Wired magazine's *Encyclopedia of the New Economy*: http://hotwired.lycos.com/special/ene/

Wolfe, T. (1990) *The Bonfire of the Vanities.* Picador, London.

World Bank (1999) *World Development Report: Knowledge for Development.* World Bank, Washington D.C.

Wrath, K. (2001) 'It's the knowledge economy, stupid'. *Unlimited.* August 2001. 76.

Zuboff, S. (1988) *In the Age of the Smart Machine: The Future of Work and Power.* Basic Books, New York.

Index

accounting, and knowledge, 19-22, 37-41
acquisition of knowledge, 90-91
adaptation, organisational, 91-92
Amazon.com, 24, 143
America-On-Line (AOL), 19
analysis, techniques of, 41-44
Andersen Consulting, 60
applying knowledge, 14, 114, 115-116, 135-136
Argyris, Chris, 108, 111
assets, tangible vs intangible, 19-22, 37-41
auditory learners, 108-109
awards for knowledge-sharing, 62, 91, 99, 134-135, 154

benchmarking, external, 149, 169
Boyle, David, 37, 38, 41, 43, 64
'brain gain', 21, 39-40
Brown, J.S. and Duguid, P., 17, 23, 24, 55, 63, 95
business development, 149

Campbell, Todd, 77
career paths, 160-161
Center for Workforce Development, 95
Chief Knowledge Officer, 158-159, 170
communication, 41-44, 71, 81-82, 86, 168
 - see also informal organisation; knowledge sharing / transfer
communities of practice, 95-97, 147
competency maps, 93-94
competitive advantage, 11, 12, 17-30, 32-33, 153

computers - see information technology
conceptualisation, 41-44
confidentiality, 130, 138
consultants, 91, 130, 171
content management, 85, 86, 148-149
Corich, Katherine, 146
Coupland, Douglas, *Generation X*, 72
creative abrasion, 104
creative thinking, 111
culture, organisational, 78-79, 88-89, 90, 92, 101, 102-103, 144, 151-154
customer/supplier capital, 61, 67-68, 119

data, 75, 79 - see also information; knowledge
 definitions of, 51-52, 53, 55, 57-60
 reduction of knowledge to, 60, 81
 sources, identifying, 126-128
'data reduction', 76
databases, 80-82, 89, 126-128, 148-149
Davenport, T. and Beck, J. *The Attention Economy*, 43, 85, 94, 98, 167, 169
Davenport, T. and Prusak, L., 21, 27, 48, 51, 52, 54, 55, 62, 70, 71, 82, 90, 96, 103, 105, 106, 148, 159, 166
decision-making, naturalistic, 64
dedicated resources, 91
Denning, Stephen, 31, 32, 42, 95, 101, 125, 157
DNA (define, nurture, allocate) management approach, 150, 156-157
documentary knowledge, 126-128, 148
DocuShare, 83

189

dotcoms, 19–20, 21
Drucker, Peter, 22, 52, 143–144, 150, 152–153, 155
dumbing down, 38
Dying for information, 75

e-commerce, 142–143 – *see also* dotcoms
e-mail, 74, 84, 85, 156, 166
Edvinsson, Leif, 40, 41, 66
end users of information technology, 76–79, 82–87, 102, 119
explicit knowledge, 63, 64, 65, 118, 126–128

fads, 48–49
Field of Dreams, 76–79
focus groups, 121, 125–126, 130
Ford Motor Company, 97
frequently-asked-questions (FAQ), 131–132, 148
Fukuyama, Francis, 106
fusion, 91, 104
FYI, 84–85

'gap analysis', 127–128
GAP-ACT system, 67
Garvin, David, 154
Gleick, James, 28, 29, 42
globalisation, impetus of, 27
glossary, 102
goals, strategic, 33, 46, 149, 164–165
groupware, 83, 166

Handy, Charles, 30, 34, 107, 108
Hewlett Packard, 102
human capital, 39, 61, 62–66, 93, 118 – *see also* staff management
human resources management – *see* staff management

I-R-S-A knowledge management strategy, 114–140
IBM, 20, 21, 91
identification of knowledge assets, 14, 19–22, 114, 115, 118–123
induction, 145
informal organisation, 82, 92, 95–97, 100–101, 133–134, 147, 156 – *see also* tacit knowledge
information – *see also* data; knowledge
  availability of, 28–29
  definitions of, 52–53, 55, 57–60
  quality of, 79, 85
  timeliness of, 79
information economy, 17–30, 34–37
'information overload', 75, 84
information superhighway, 18
information technology – *see also* computers; end users
  effect on human ability to reason and remember, 81–82
  in mature knowledge management organisations, 148–149
  knowledge management and, 13, 69–87, 88–89, 166–167
  productivity and, 24–25, 71–76
  proliferation of, 27–28
Information Technology Advisory Group (ITAG), 22–23
intellectual capital, 60–68 – *see also* knowledge
intellectual property, 62
intelligence skills, 109–110
Internet, 22, 24, 29, 142–145
intranets, 28, 60, 70, 80–81, 82, 86, 97, 167
inventory, knowledge replaces, 143
Iyer, Pico, 27, 74

Jonscher, Charles, 19, 24, 25, 28, 50–51, 52, 57, 64, 71, 72, 73, 74, 79, 87
just-in-time delivery, 84, 87, 143, 160

Kim, C. and Mauborgne, R., 150, 156, 158
knowledge, 34–37, 88–89 – *see also* data; information; wisdom
  accounting and, 19–22, 37–41
  acquisition of, 90–91
  definitions of, 53–60
  explicit, 63, 64, 65, 118, 126–128
  missing, 65–66
  operational levels of, 55–57
  production and distribution of, 18
  renting of, 91
  social networks of, 82, 92, 96–97, 100–101, 133–134, 147, 156
  tacit, 63–65, 118, 123–126

INDEX

Knowledge Capital Scoreboard, 40
knowledge economy, 17–30, 34–37
'knowledge fairs', 101, 134, 147
knowledge flows, 89–90, 99–104
knowledge leaders, 102
knowledge management
   benefits of, 45–46, 169
   definitions of, 11–12, 31–33, 50–51
   getting started, 162–171
   I-R-S-A strategy, 114–140
   information technology and, 13, 69–87, 88–89
   key elements of, 88–113
   mature, 141–161
   poor, symptoms of, 12
   process of, 114–117
   value of starting small, 139–140, 162
   what not to do, 170–171
knowledge manager, 134, 154–159
knowledge maps, 82–83, 100, 119–123, 131–132, 148, 164
knowledge marketplace, 104–107
knowledge organisation, 142–154
knowledge repositories, 120–122
knowledge sharing / transfer, 11, 12, 32, 80–81, 82–83, 92–93, 99–107
   awards for, 62, 91, 99, 134–135
   educating staff about value of, 162–163
   I-R-S-A strategy, 14, 114, 115, 129–135
   novel methods of, 168–169
knowledge stocks, 89–99
knowledge workers – see staff management

language, common, 101–102
leaders, 102
learning, 13, 70, 86, 95–96, 107–112, 137, 145, 154, 166
   in mature knowledge management organisation, 145, 147–148
   styles of, 108–109
libraries, 80, 89
Lotus Notes, 82, 83

management, workplace, 150, 152–153, 155–159 – see also staff management
memory, human, effect of information technology on, 81–82

mentoring, 80, 106, 146
'meta-knowledge' analysis, 127, 128, 130
microchips, 22, 27–28
Microsoft, 19, 20, 21, 37, 98
missing knowledge, 65–66
Moore's Law, 27–28
Most Admired Knowledge Enterprises (MAKE) award, 154
multiple intelligences, 109–110

narrative techniques of analysis and communication, 42–43, 125, 132–133
National Security Agency, 75–76
naturalistic decision-making, 64
Navigator system, 40
networks, informal, 82, 92, 96–97, 100–101, 133–134, 147, 156
New Zealand
   knowledge economy, 18, 22–23
   managing the 'knowledge wave', 46–47
   rewards for knowledge workers, 98–99
Noam, Eli, 76
Nonaka, Ikujiro, 153
'Not Invented Here, But I Did it Anyway' award, 62, 91

office layout, 101, 148
organisation, informal, 82, 92, 95–97, 100–101, 133–134, 147, 156 – see also tacit knowledge
organisational change, 29–30, 47, 141, 154–158, 159–161
organisational culture, 78–79, 88–89, 90, 92, 101, 102–103, 144, 151–154
organisational learning, 13, 70, 86, 95–96, 107–112, 137, 154, 166
   in mature knowledge management organisation, 145, 147–148
organisational performance, 14, 44–47
organisational structures / processes, 143–150

Parker, Ian, 74
path dependency, 69–70
performance, organisational, 14, 44–47, 149–150
performance, staff, 145–146
Pfeffer, J. and Sutton, R., 95

Philips Fox, 80-81
pilot four-phase knowledge management project, 163-164
power, 11, 12, 17-30, 32-33
premises, knowledge replaces, 142-143
production, knowledge replaces, 142
productivity and information technology, 24-25, 71-76

reciprocity, 105-106
reflection about organisational knowledge, 14, 114, 115, 123-129
remuneration of staff, 97-98, 99, 145
renting knowledge, 91
Reuters, 75
Ris, Ian, 48
risk management, 137-139
Rollo, C. and Clark, T., 28, 35, 45, 79
Roszak, Theodore, *The Cult of Information*, 72

secondary source analysis, 126-128
Semler, Ricardo, 133, 155
service sector, 159-160
sharing of knowledge - *see* knowledge sharing / transfer
Shenk, David, *Data Smog*, 18, 29, 76, 87
skills of staff, 93, 94, 109-110, 137, 161 - *see also* training of staff
'snowball' sampling method, 120
social constructionism, 25, 77-78
social exchange theory, 105
Solow, Robert, 25, 71
staff improvement systems (SIS), 94-95
staff management, 13, 17, 19-20, 92-113, 165-166 - *see also* end users of information technology; human capital; productivity; workplace culture
  in mature knowledge management organisation, 144-146
  recruitment, 98-99, 144
  rewards, 97-98, 99, 145
Stewart, Thomas, *Intellectual Capital*, 20, 35, 36, 38, 39, 60-61, 65, 67, 80, 92, 93, 96, 98, 141, 143, 155, 159, 160, 165

storytelling, 42-43, 125, 132-133
strategic goals / planning, 33, 46, 149, 164-165 - *see also* I-R-S-A strategy
structural capital, 61, 66-67, 118
succession planning, 146
Sun Microsystems, 151, 152, 157
supplier capital, 61, 67-68, 119
Sveiby, Karl, 40, 41

tacit knowledge, 63-65, 118, 123-126
  converting to explicit knowledge, 124-126, 153
tactile / kinaesthetic learners, 109
talk spaces, 100, 101, 134, 147, 148
technological determinism, 25, 77-78
Tenner, Edward, 24, 72, 73, 78
tension, creative, 104
thesaurus, 102
'thirty-three-and-a-third rule', 70
360-degree review process, 120, 164
training of staff, 93-94, 145, 162-163, 167 - *see also* skills of staff
trust, 106-107

visual learners, 108

Williamson, Trevor, 31, 47
wisdom, 57-60
work, changing nature of, 29-30, 159-161
workplace culture, 78-79, 88-89, 90, 92, 101, 102-103, 144, 151-154
workplace management, 150, 152-153, 155-159

Xerox, 37, 71, 83, 100-101

'Yellow Pages', 82-83, 100, 119-123, 131-132, 148, 164

Zuboff, Shoshana, *In the Age of the Smart Machine*, 157-158